HEALTH CARE IN TRANSITION

MEDICAID PRESCRIPTION DRUGS

PRICING AND POLICY ISSUES

Health Care in Transition

Additional books in this series can be found on Nova's website under the Series tab.

Additional e-books in this series can be found on Nova's website under the e-book tab.

HEALTH CARE IN TRANSITION

MEDICAID PRESCRIPTION DRUGS

PRICING AND POLICY ISSUES

SANDRA OLIVIA BARTON
EDITOR

nova publishers
New York

Library of Congress Cataloging-in-Publication Data

ISBN: 978-1-63482-522-1

Published by Nova Science Publishers, Inc. † New York

CONTENTS

PREFACE

This book discusses Medicaid prescription drug pricing and policies.

Chapter 1 – Medicaid is a federal-state entitlement program that pays for health care and related services on behalf of certain low-income individuals. Prescription drugs are an optional Medicaid benefit and all states cover outpatient drugs. States can create formularies, or lists of preferred drugs, but federal rules tend to result in comprehensive coverage, even for beneficiaries enrolled in Medicaid managed care plans. Pharmaceutical manufacturers that voluntarily participate in Medicaid are required to pay rebates to states on covered outpatient drugs, which help Medicaid receive manufacturers' lowest or best price. States then share the rebate they receive from pharmaceutical manufacturers with the federal government.

This report discusses how Medicaid pays for drugs, including statutory requirements on manufacturers and states as well as a number of regulations and policies that help to administer the program.

Chapter 2 – States reimburse pharmacies for covered outpatient prescription drugs dispensed to Medicaid beneficiaries. For certain multiple-source outpatient prescription drugs, federal matching funds that states receive to reimburse pharmacies are limited by FULs. In 2010, PPACA modified the FUL formula to better reflect pharmacy acquisition costs and thus more effectively control Medicaid expenditures. However, CMS has not yet implemented the PPACA formula and continues to use FULs that were published in September 2009. CMS currently publishes draft PPACA-based FULs. CMS also created the NADACs for states to consider when setting reimbursement rates.

In: Medicaid Prescription Drugs
Editor: Sandra Olivia Barton

ISBN: 978-1-63482-522-1

Chapter 1

MEDICAID PRESCRIPTION DRUG PRICING AND POLICY*

Cliff Binder

SUMMARY

Medicaid is a federal-state entitlement program that pays for health care and related services on behalf of certain low-income individuals. Prescription drugs are an optional Medicaid benefit and all states cover outpatient drugs. States can create formularies, or lists of preferred drugs, but federal rules tend to result in comprehensive coverage, even for beneficiaries enrolled in Medicaid managed care plans. Pharmaceutical manufacturers that voluntarily participate in Medicaid are required to pay rebates to states on covered outpatient drugs, which help Medicaid receive manufacturers' lowest or *best price*. States then share the rebate they receive from pharmaceutical manufacturers with the federal government.

In determining the amount of rebate, Medicaid law distinguishes between the following two drug types: (1) single source drugs (brand-name drugs) and innovator multiple source drugs (brand-name drugs that now have generic competition); and (2) all other, non-innovator, multiple source (generic) drugs. Rebates for the first category of drugs—drugs still under patent or those once covered by patents—have two components: a basic rebate and an additional

* This is an edited, reformatted and augmented version of a Congressional Research Service publication, No. R43778, dated November 7, 2014.

rebate. In addition to basic and additional rebates, most states negotiate supplemental rebates with drug manufacturers, by offering to encourage use of a manufacturer's product in exchange for a price concession (rebate).

States, through retail pharmacies, purchase drugs on behalf of Medicaid beneficiaries. Medicaid pharmacy reimbursement has two components: a payment to cover the cost of the pharmacy buying the drug (ingredient cost) and a payment for the pharmacist's services in filling a prescription (dispensing fee). States set reimbursement for both ingredient costs and dispensing fees.

In FY2005, Medicaid fee-for-service (FFS) drug expenditures were approximately $43.1 billion, but by FY2013 had decreased to $19.8 billion. Over the same period, Medicaid FFS drug rebate collections were at about the same level ($12.4 billion), but managed care rebate collections increased substantially to about $4.8 billion in FY2013. The decreases in Medicaid FFS drug expenditures and the increases in rebate collections were mostly offset by at least the following other factors or trends: (1) Beginning January 1, 2006, prescription drug coverage of individuals eligible for both Medicare and Medicaid (dual eligibles) was moved from Medicaid to Medicare Part D which resulted in substantially reduced Medicaid FFS drug spending. Due to maintenance of effort requirements, state Medicaid programs continue to pay the vast majority of dual eligible drug costs, even though those expenditures are not counted as drug spending. (2) Statutory changes helped to increased rebate collections by extending rebates to Medicaid enrollees covered by managed care plans and increasing the amount of rebates owed by drug companies. (3) The loss of patent protection for a number of commonly prescribed drugs further contributed to decreasing Medicaid drug expenditures. And (4) the rapid shift in enrollment of beneficiaries to managed care plans that cover prescription drugs.

In December 2013, Solvaldi®, a new brand-name drug, was approved by the Food and Drug Administration for treatment of hepatitis virus C (HVC) infections. Solvaldi® is estimated to cost $1,000 per pill, and total treatment cost estimates range from $84,000 to more than $168,000. The rebates states and the federal government receive will help reduce Medicaid's Solvaldi® expenditures, but until other equivalent drugs are available to increase competition, states may have limited leverage to negotiate additional manufacturer price concessions. Medicaid rebates, however, while buffering the cost of prescription drugs, might also contribute to drug manufacturers setting increasingly higher launch prices.

The current Medicaid drug pricing and policy infrastructure was designed for FFS, and may not work as well with significant managed care enrollment. Under managed care contracts, states generally delegate some or all of drug utilization review and individual drug claim oversight to plans, including program integrity. With managed care and pharmaceutical benefit managers (PBMs) responsible for these activities, states have responsibility for ensuring plans uphold their contract obligations. States' prescription drug monitoring is tailored to FFS drug claims. It is unclear how much oversight of managed care claims states will be able to provide. If states and the federal government currently procure drugs for Medicaid beneficiaries at some of the lowest prices, will it be possible for managed care plans to further reduce costs without imposing barriers to Medicaid beneficiaries in obtaining covered drugs?

EXECUTIVE SUMMARY

Medicaid is a federal-state entitlement program that pays for health care and related services on behalf of certain low-income individuals. All states participate in Medicaid, but participation is not required. If states participate, then under federal Medicaid law they are required to provide health service benefits to certain individuals—mandatory eligibility groups—but states have the option of covering other groups too. Similarly, states must cover certain services for mandatory eligibility groups, but they have the option to cover fewer services for other eligibility groups. In general, Medicaid health benefits are broad for mandatory eligibility groups, but more restricted for other eligibility groups. Prescription drugs are an optional Medicaid benefit, but all states cover outpatient drugs. States may create formularies, lists of preferred drugs, but federal rules tend to result in comprehensive coverage, even for beneficiaries enrolled in Medicaid managed care plans.

Medicaid Managed Care[1]

Medicaid managed care differs from traditional fee-forservice (FFS) health services delivery in that state Medicaid programs prospectively pay a managed care plan a fixed monthly amount for each Medicaid enrollee, regardless of whether or not the beneficiary needed health services during the month.

> If the cost of health services required by Medicaid managed care beneficiaries are less than states monthly payments (capitation), the managed care plan keeps the difference. If the cost of treating beneficiaries exceed state monthly payments, the managed care plan is responsible for the additional costs.
>
> States may offer Medicaid beneficiaries the option to enroll in a managed care plan or they may mandate that all or certain beneficiaries enroll in managed care plans.

Since 1990, pharmaceutical manufacturers who voluntarily agree to participate in Medicaid are required to rebate a portion of drug payments back to states. When a manufacturer participates in Medicaid, states must make most of their drugs available to Medicaid beneficiaries. States share the rebates they receive from drug manufacturers with the federal government. The drug rebates required under federal law help the state and federal Medicaid program receive manufacturers' lowest or *best price*. Beginning in 2010, drug manufacturers also were required to pay rebates on drugs provided to Medicaid beneficiaries enrolled in managed care.

Medicaid Prescription Drug Reimbursement

For the purpose of determining rebates, Medicaid distinguishes between two drug types: (1) single source drugs (generally, those still under patent) and innovator multiple source drugs (drugs originally marketed under a patent or original new drug application but for which there now are generic equivalents); and (2) all other, non-innovator, multiple source drugs. Rebates for the first category of drugs—drugs still under patent or those once covered by patents—have two components: a basic rebate and an additional rebate. Medicaid's basic rebate for single source and innovator multiple source drugs is the larger of either the difference between a drug's quarterly average manufacturer price (AMP) and the *best price* for the same period, or a flat percentage (23.1%) of the drug's quarterly AMP.[2] Drug manufacturers owe an additional rebate when their unit prices for individual products increased faster than inflation. For all other drugs, the rebate is a flat percentage (13%) of a drug's quarterly AMP. States separately negotiate additional, supplemental, rebates with drug manufacturers in exchange for listing manufacturer products on the state's preferred drug list.[3]

State Medicaid agencies reimburse retail pharmacies for covered outpatient prescription drugs dispensed to Medicaid beneficiaries. Medicaid FFS payments to pharmacies for outpatient prescription drugs have two components: a payment to cover the cost of the pharmacy buying the drug (the ingredient cost) and a payment for the pharmacist's professional services in filling and dispensing the prescription (the dispensing fee).[4] States, subject to the Centers for Medicare & Medicaid Services (CMS) approval, set reimbursement amounts for both ingredient costs and dispensing fees. Dispensing fees usually are a fixed amount, intended to cover the procuring and storing drugs, consultation, and dispensing drugs. The ingredient cost component of the pharmacy payment is an approximation of a drug's market price which is intended to reimburse the pharmacy for the cost of acquiring the drug. To encourage substitution of lower-cost generic equivalent drugs for more expensive sole source drugs, federal law requires CMS to set a maximum on what it will pay for certain multiple source drug ingredients. The maximum multiple drug ingredient payments are called federal upper limits (FULs).

Drug Expenditures and Trends

Based on state FY2013 Medicaid financial reports, Medicaid FFS outpatient prescription drug expenditures, net of federal and state rebates, were $16.2 billion, down from $30.7 billion in FY2005 (Figure 1). However, decreases in Medicaid FFS drug expenditures do not represent an overall decrease in Medicaid prescription drug expenditures, because there have been prescription drug industry trends as well as a number of statutory changes that have shifted Medicaid drug expenditures to other spending accounts. For instance, beginning January 1, 2006, prescription drug coverage of disabled and elderly Medicaid beneficiaries—those covered by both Medicare and Medicaid (dual eligibles)—was moved from Medicaid to Medicare Part D. Dual eligibles accounted for a considerable portion of Medicaid drug expenditures, and as a result, when they were moved to Medicare Part D, Medicaid drug expenditures decreased. A maintenance of effort (MOE) provision in federal Medicare law required states to continue to pay the vast majority of dual eligible drug costs.[5]

Another factor that contributed to the decline in FFS drug expenditures is the recent escalation in the movement of Medicaid beneficiary drug coverage from FFS to managed care contracts that include drug coverage. One indicator of the movement to managed care coverage of drugs was the growth in managed care rebates, which were required beginning in FY2010. In FY2011, states collected $932 million (national and state supplemental rebates) in managed care rebates, which increased to $4.7 billion in FY2013 (Table 5). Another indicator of the migration to managed care is the change in the number of FFS drug claims which declined by almost 25% between FY2011-FY2012 (Table C-1). Decreased drug claims for five states accounted for over 90% of the decrease.[6] The statutory changes helped to increase overall rebate collections which had the effect of reducing net drug expenditures. States reported collecting a total of $11.7 billion in federally required FFS rebates and an additional $726 million in state FFS supplemental drug rebates, and $4.7 billion in managed care rebates for a total of $17.2 billion in FY2013—Table 7 and Table 6). Other factors that contributed to the decline in FFS drug expenditures were drug industry trends and changes in Medicaid laws applicable to prescription drugs. The drug industry patent cliff, where a number of block buster drugs came off patent over a few years, reduced Medicaid FFS drug costs as these drugs became available as cheaper generic products.

Selected other Medicaid FFS prescription drug data show that average FY2013 per-person Medicaid prescription drug expenditures were just over $926 (Table 11) down from $1,509 in FY2005. In FY2012, Medicaid on average paid approximately $282 for single source prescription drug claims, $149 for innovator multiple source claims, and $18 for non-innovator multiple source drug claim (Table 12). Medicaid's generic prescribing rate for all states varies; the national average in FY2012 was 76% (Table D-1).

Medicaid Prescription Drug Issues

The Patient Protection and Affordable Care Act (ACA, P.L. 111-148) made a number of modifications to federal Medicaid law. The CMS published a proposed rule that provided guidance on implementation of the ACA changes in February 2012. A final rule that would codify many of the new Medicaid drug requirements is pending as of the date of this report. In December 2013, Solvaldi® a new brand name drug was approved by the Food and Drug Administration for treatment of hepatitis virus C (HVC) infections.

Solvaldi® was estimated to cost $1,000 per pill and total treatment cost estimates can range from $84,000 to more than $168,000.[7] Through federal health programs, including Medicaid's prescription drug benefit, federal and state governments may pay the majority of HVC treatment costs. Solvaldi® has raised an issue because of its high price and that many individuals with HCV infections are covered by Medicaid.[8] For Medicaid, states and the federal government will receive rebates for Solvaldi® that will help reduce the drug's cost, but until other equivalent drugs are available to increase competition, states may have limited leverage to negotiate additional manufacturer price concessions. Medicaid rebates, while buffering the cost of prescription drugs somewhat, might also contribute to drug manufacturers setting increasingly higher launch prices.

Conclusion

Medicaid's drug pricing and policy have been effective in helping to control Medicaid FFS drug expenditures. Outpatient drug expenditures have decreased and Medicaid is able to buy drugs for lower prices than Medicare Part D plans, the other major federal outpatient prescription drug purchaser. Congress has been instrumental in establishing state and federal authority to ensure Medicaid receives manufacturers' lowest prescription drug prices. Congress authorized creation of Medicaid program infrastructure to manage, monitor, and enforce prescription drug pricing. However, if the pace in the movement of Medicaid enrollees to managed care that includes prescription drug benefits continues, then prescription drug oversight may be more difficult. The current Medicaid drug pricing and policy infrastructure was designed for FFS, and may not work as well with significant managed care enrollment. States have authority to collect rebates under managed care arrangements, although how state supplemental rebates will align with managed care plan drug discount negotiations is unclear. Under managed care contracts, states generally delegate some or all of drug utilization review and individual drug claim oversight to plans, including program integrity. When managed care and PBMs are responsible for these activities, states have responsibility for ensuring plans uphold their contract obligations.[9] States' prescription drug monitoring is tailored to FFS drug claims, and it is unclear how much oversight of managed care claims states will be able to provide. If states and the federal government currently procure drugs for Medicaid beneficiaries at some of the lowest prices, will it be possible for managed care plans and PBMs, to further reduce costs without imposing barriers to Medicaid beneficiaries in obtain covered drugs?

OVERVIEW

Medicaid drug pricing and policy is complex, in part because prescription drug markets are dynamic. Drug manufacturers and wholesalers adapt to policy and statutory changes by creating new products and new marketing approaches that sometimes circumvent Medicaid pricing rules. Drug companies and health insurers operate in private markets in which they are seeking private advantages to earn revenue and profits. Medicaid pricing policies are, in part, based on competitive market transactions. Even though Medicaid buys drugs through the same markets as other payers, federal law requires drug companies, operating through wholesalers and distributors, to sell drugs to Medicaid at discounted prices. Medicaid's drug discounts vary depending on whether drugs are available from one manufacturer—single source—or are available from two or more manufacturers—multiple source. Single source drug discounts are greater than multiple source drug discounts. In 2010, the Congressional Budget Office (CBO) estimated that total single source Medicaid drug rebates averaged approximately 57% of manufacturers' average prices.[10]

This report discusses how Medicaid pays for drugs, including statutory requirements on manufacturers and states as well as a number of regulations and policies that help to administer the program. Medicaid beneficiaries are dispensed drugs at retail pharmacies, but states pay most of the cost of those drugs. States then receive discounts from drug manufacturers in the form of rebate payments, which state share with the federal government through a credit against states' future Medicaid payments. Since 2006, the amount states and the federal government have spent on drugs for beneficiaries enrolled in fee-for-service (FFS) Medicaid has decreased whereas the amount states have collected from rebates has increased.

The focus of this report is on FFS prescription drug pricing and policy. FFS drug spending accounted for the vast majority of Medicaid drug purchases in 2010 with CBO estimating that prescription drug purchases on behalf of Medicaid beneficiaries enrolled in managed care contracts represented approximately 10% of Medicaid drug expenditures.[11] However, Medicaid managed care contracts including prescription drug coverage have grown very rapidly since FY2010. Data for Medicaid managed care drug expenditures are not as readily available as those for FFS drug spending because those expenditures are not separately reported on Medicaid financial reporting forms.

Nonetheless, when possible or appropriate, information on managed care prescription drug spending and utilization are included in the discussion in this report, but in general managed care drug expenditures and utilization are outside its scope. There is considerable Medicaid and related health expenditure data present throughout this report. These data are nominal and have not been inflation adjusted.

A number of Medicaid drug pricing terms are commonly abbreviated. **Table 1** displays many of the Medicaid drug-related acronyms and abbreviations that appear in this report. In addition, **Table 2** displays a list of public laws referenced throughout the report, and **Table E-1** in **Appendix E** is a glossary of selected Medicaid drug terms.

Table 1. Selected Medicaid Drug and Other Acronyms

Acronym	Term	Acronym	Term
AAC	Actual Acquisition Cost	MSIS	Medicaid Statistical Information System
AMP	Average Manufacturer Price	NADAC	National Average Drug Acquisition Cost
BOE	Basis of Eligibility	PBM	Pharmaceutical Benefit Management
CMS	Centers for Medicare & Medicaid Services	PCCM	Primary Care Case Management
DOD	Department of Defense	PSC	Phased-down State Contribution
DUR	Drug Utilization Review	PHS	Public Health Service
EAC	Estimated Acquisition Cost	OTC	Over-the-Counter
FEHBP	Federal Employees Health Benefit Program	RCP	Retail Community Pharmacy
FFS	Fee-for-Service	SPA	State Plan Amendment
FUL	Federal Upper Limit	SRA	Supplemental Rebate Agreement
FMAP	Federal Medical Assistance Percentage	WAC	Wholesale Acquisition Cost
MAC	Maximum Allowable Cost	VHA	Veterans Health Administration

Table 2. Public Laws Referenced in This Report

Abbreviation	Public Law	Number
ACA	Patient Protection and Affordable Care Act	P.L. 111-148
ARRA	American Recovery and Reinvestment Act of 2009	P.L. 111-5
DRA	Deficit Reduction Act of 2005	P.L. 109-171
EJMAA	Education, Jobs, and Medicaid Assistance Act	P.L. 111-226
MIPPA	Medicare Improvements for Patients and Providers of 2008	P.L. 110-275
MMA	Medicare Prescription Drug, Improvement, and Modernization Act of 2003	P.L. 108-173
OBRA90	Omnibus Budget Reconciliation Act of 1990	P.L. 101-508
—	QI, TMA and Abstinence Programs Extension and Hurricane Katrina	P.L. 109-91
	Unemployment Relief Act of 2005	
SSA	Social Security Act	—
VHCA	Veterans Health Care Act of 1992	P.L. 102-585

Medicaid Program Basics

Medicaid is a federal-state entitlement program that pays for medical services on behalf of certain low-income individuals. The Centers for Medicare & Medicaid Services (CMS) administers the Medicaid program under authority delegated by the Secretary of the Department of Health and Human Services (the Secretary).[12] Estimated FY2013 federal expenditures for Medicaid benefits and administration were approximately $262 billion; state expenditures were estimated to be an additional $192 billion, for a total program cost of approximately $454 billion.[13]

State Medicaid programs are administered and designed by the states under broad federal guidelines.[14] All states elect to participate in Medicaid, so they are required to provide benefits to certain low-income individuals and optionally may cover other individuals.[15] Similarly, states must cover certain basic services, but may also cover additional services. States set their provider payment rates for medical and related services, subject to limitations and federal approval. There is considerable variation across states, with some programs being relatively limited and others more generous in terms of eligible populations, covered benefits, and service payments.

Medicaid is a means-tested program. Enrollees' income and other resources must be within program financial standards.[16] These standards vary among states and among different population groups within a state. With some exceptions, Medicaid is available only to very low income individuals—most Medicaid enrollees have incomes below the federal poverty level (FPL).[17] Until recently, Medicaid was primarily available only to children, adult members of families with children, pregnant women, and aged, blind, or disabled individuals. People outside those categories—such as single adults and childless couples—generally did not qualify for Medicaid regardless of their income level.[18] ACA permitted states to expand Medicaid coverage to single adults up to age 65 provided their income did not exceed 133% of FPL and required states to cover mandatory eligibility groups up to 133% of FPL.[19]

Historically, Medicaid eligibility groups were divided into two basic classes, the categorically needy and the medically needy. These classes differentiated between beneficiaries who were eligible for Medicaid because their income was low (categorically needy) and those who were eligible because they had high medical expenses (medically needy). Categorically needy Medicaid beneficiaries received cash-assistance payments (welfare), so their eligibility was considered welfare-related. Categorically needy beneficiaries represent the majority of Medicaid beneficiaries.

Although their income may have exceeded states' Medicaid income eligibility threshold, medically needy beneficiaries were eligible for Medicaid because a high percentage of that income was used to pay medical expenses, which left only a small amount of income for other living expenses. In 2009, 33 states covered medically needy individuals and these individuals accounted for approximately 5% of national Medicaid enrollment, and 11% of Medicaid expenditures (about $37 billion).[20]

Over time, more categorically needy eligibility groups were added. As a result, distinctions between categorically and medically needy eligibility became less useful in identifying which groups qualified for mandatory or optional benefits. Nonetheless, the distinctions are useful when considering certain benefits.[21] Most benefits are considered mandatory only for categorically needy individuals; that is, states must cover those benefits for the categorically needy but they are an option for medically needy individuals. Other benefits, including outpatient prescription drugs, are optional for both groups of beneficiaries. Some states provide those optional benefits only to categorically needy individuals whereas other states provide optional benefits to one or more medically needy groups as well.[22]

Medicaid Prescription Drug Benefits

Coverage of outpatient prescription drugs is optional for state Medicaid programs. All states cover outpatient prescription drugs for mandatory (categorically needy) eligibility groups, but they may not cover drugs for optional groups (including medically needy) and drug coverage for expansion populations may be limited to either benchmark plan coverage or a particular set of drugs.[23,24] Most states cover outpatient drugs because these drugs are considered a lower-cost alternative to other medical care. Prescription drugs may help keep enrollees healthier and potentially prevent more serious and more costly medical interventions.[25]

In general, Medicaid FFS and managed care outpatient drug benefits are broad, encompassing most prescription drugs and many non-prescription, over-the-counter (OTC), drugs. Medicaid prescription drug coverage is broad because Medicaid law requires states to cover most drugs offered by manufacturers that have rebate agreements in effect. In addition, federal law permits states to use formularies to direct beneficiaries to equivalent lower-cost drugs, but there also must be a process by which health care providers may request covered drugs not on the formulary if the provider determines those drugs are medically necessary.[26] When states contract with managed care plans and drug coverage is included, the plans may use their own formularies but also must have a process by which health care providers can prescribe non-formulary drugs that they determine are medically necessary.

Fee-for-Service Coverage

For Medicaid beneficiaries enrolled in FFS Medicaid, federal statute allows states to establish formularies. Formularies are lists of drugs that payers prefer to have prescribed to beneficiaries, generally because these drugs cost less and are considered by experts to be as safe and effective as other drug choices. When private health care insurers or providers cover only those drugs on the list and deny payment for others, the list is referred to as a *closed formulary*. Medicaid formularies are seldom as restrictive as the closed formularies found in the private insurance market because of two statutory requirements. The first requirement is that states must cover any non-formulary drug (with the exception of certain drugs) that is specifically requested and approved through a prior authorization process.[27] The second requirement is that states cover all drugs offered by manufacturers that entered into rebate agreements with the Secretary. States may use formularies to exclude drugs for which there are no significant therapeutic advantages over other drugs that are included in the formularies, as long as there is a publicly available explanation for a drug's exclusion.[28]

Although federal law ensures Medicaid formularies are not too restrictive, it also allows states to exclude certain drugs, drug classes, or drug uses from Medicaid coverage.[29] States may still cover excluded drugs and receive federal financial participation (FFP) for them.[30] Medicaid-excluded drugs are not subject to the requirement that states must cover all of a manufacturer's products if the manufacturer entered into a Medicaid rebate agreement with the Secretary. Federal Medicaid law also requires states to cover three additional drugs, drug classes, or their medical uses.[31]

Medicaid Managed Care Drug Coverage

Many Medicaid managed care arrangements are limited risk-based contracts that rely on primary care case management (PCCM). Under PCCM and similar limited-risk contracts, Medicaid programs pay providers a small fixed fee to manage patients' care.[32] Further, in PCCM and other non-risk bearing managed care arrangements, prescription drug benefits generally are delivered and reimbursed as FFS Medicaid benefits.

For Medicaid beneficiaries enrolled in managed care plans, or plans to which states pay a fixed monthly capitation payment in exchange for the provision of all or some subset of covered services, Medicaid statute permits those managed care plans an exception from the FFS drug coverage rules described above.[33] When state Medicaid programs cover drugs or other services, such as mental health or long-term care services and supports, through managed care contracts, the services covered are considered *carved in* to the managed care contracts. When states do not cover drug benefits or other services, those services are considered *carved out* of the managed care contracts. Medicaid law allows managed care plans to develop and administer drug formularies. In practice, however, when prescription drugs are covered under capitated managed care contracts, states sometimes require managed care plans to have the same coverage and formulary limits as FFS Medicaid coverage.[34] Only some managed care contracts include prescription drug benefits, although increasingly more include drug coverage. Since 2010, as states have moved to carve-in prescription drug coverage, more states now permit managed care plans to use their own formularies.[35] Even if states delegate formulary decisions to managed care plans, the plans must still provide access to all Medicaid covered drugs, just as required under FFS Medicaid. Medicaid managed care plans may reimburse the retail pharmacy, similar to FFS Medicaid, or they can provide outpatient drugs directly to beneficiaries.

As shown in **Table 3**, even though the Medicaid managed care enrollment percentage was over 70% in 2011 (for any managed care) these arrangements accounted for only about 25% of Medicaid benefit expenditures, which include drug expenditures.

Table 3. Percentage of Medicaid Managed Care Enrollment and Benefit Expenditures FY2008 and FY2011

	Enrollee Percentage		Benefit Spending Percentage	
Managed Care Arrangement	FY2008	FY2011	FY2008	FY2011
Any Managed Care	61.5%	71.8%	21.1%	25.3%
Comprehensive Risk-Based Managed Care	46.8%	49.8%	18.2%	23.9%

Source: The Medicaid and CHIP Payment and Access Commission (MACPAC), Report to the Congress, *The Evolution of Managed Care in Medicaid*, June 2011, Table 9 and 12; and June 2014, Table 14 and 15.

Similarly, 2011 Medicaid benefit expenditures for comprehensive risk-based managed care contracts accounted for about 50% of enrollment but constituted only slightly less than 24% of benefit expenditures, including drug expenditures. Table 3 also displays the Medicaid managed care enrollment increase between FY2008 and FY2011, with rising percentages going to both any managed care and comprehensive risk-based arrangements. Managed care was estimated to account for about 10% of Medicaid prescription drug expenditures in 2010, a figure that was estimated to have increased to approximately 50% in 2013.[36]

OTC Drugs

Many state Medicaid programs also cover OTC drugs, those medications that can be purchased without a prescription. In 2007, all states covered some OTC drugs, although no state covered all OTC drugs and most states limited coverage or imposed coverage restrictions on OTC drugs. All states covered at least some OTC drugs in the following categories: allergy, asthma, and sinus; analgesics; cough and cold; smoking cessation; digestive products; H2 antagonists; feminine products; and topical products.[37]

MEDICAID PRESCRIPTION DRUG REIMBURSEMENT

State Medicaid agencies do not purchase drugs directly from manufacturers. Instead, they most commonly reimburse retail pharmacies for covered drugs dispensed to Medicaid beneficiaries.[38] This section discusses FFS Medicaid pharmacy reimbursement issues.

Medicaid FFS Payments to Pharmacies for Prescription Drugs

Medicaid payments to pharmacies for outpatient prescription drugs have two components: a payment for what it cost pharmacists to purchase a drug (*ingredient cost*) and a payment for pharmacists' professional services in filling and dispensing prescriptions (*dispensing fee*). States, subject to CMS approval, set separate reimbursement amounts for both ingredient costs and dispensing fees. The pharmacy payment for acquiring the drug, the ingredient cost, is either an approximation of a drug's market price or the amount the pharmacy paid to buy the drug. The dispensing fee is usually a fixed amount, intended to cover drug procurement, storage, and other costs. States set their own pharmacy payments but are subject to some federal limitations. To encourage substitution of lower-cost drugs, federal Medicaid law requires the Secretary to establish a maximum payment amount for the federal share of certain multiple source drug ingredient costs—the federal upper limit (FUL).[39] The FUL program limits the federal share of Medicaid reimbursement for certain multiple source drugs and seeks to ensure that the federal government acts as a prudent buyer by taking advantage of lower market prices for these drugs.

Under Medicaid, there are two types of multiple source drugs, innovator multiple source and non-innovator multiple source drugs. Innovator multiple source drugs were initially brand-name drugs that have lost patent protection.[40] Non-innovator multiple source drugs are (1) multiple source drugs that were not initially single source products, (2) multiple source drugs that were marketed as generic products, or (3) drugs that entered the market before 1962 that were never marketed as generic drugs.[41] Brand-name drugs can be single source or innovator multiple source drugs.[42]

Generally, CMS must set an FUL amount for drugs when generic versions are available, although states must set upper limits for certain *other drugs*.[43]

Multiple Source Drug Federal Upper Limits

Federal FUL policy requires the Secretary to establish a per drug maximum for its share of Medicaid outpatient drug payments.[44] FULs are applied in aggregate to each state's spending for drugs subject to FUL limits rather than to individual prescription drug claims. Thus, a state may reimburse pharmacies at amounts above the FUL for certain drugs and not exceed the sum of FULs in aggregate if it also reimburses pharmacies at amounts below the FUL for other drugs.[45] The FUL aggregate is determined by first multiplying the FUL by the number of units dispensed of each drug. Those amounts are summed for all drugs subject to FULs, and that total represents the maximum amount eligible for FFP. Drugs subject to FULs are those the FDA has rated as having three or more therapeutically and pharmaceutically equivalent products.[46] CMS identifies drugs that are subject to FULs and then calculates the maximum payment amount for those products.[47]

The methodology for calculating FULs is to apply a percentage adjustment to the average manufacturer price (AMP) of the least costly therapeutic equivalent.[48] Under an ACA provision, the FUL percentage was decreased from the Deficit Reduction Act of 2005 (DRA, P.L. 109-171) rate of 250% of AMP to at least 175% of AMP.[49] Drug manufacturers are required under Medicaid law to report AMP.[50] AMP is defined in statute as the average price paid to the manufacturer by wholesalers for drugs distributed to retail community pharmacies (RCPs).[51] CMS has calculated and publically displayed draft FULs using the current law methodology since September 2011 but has not implemented the ACA FUL policy.[52] Thus, current FULs were based on prices in effect in 2009. CMS announced in November 2013 that it would implement the ACA FUL policy July 1, 2014.[53] However, CMS announced in June 2014 that it would delay implementation of the ACA FUL policy, but it did not indicate the length of the delay.[54]

Upper Limits for All Other Drugs

Federal Medicaid law also sets upper limits for *other drugs* a category that includes drugs for which CMS has not established a specific FUL and brand-name drugs that were *certified*.[55] Drugs that are certified include drugs for which a generic alternative is available, but the beneficiary's physician has specified that a brand name is medically necessary. The FUL for other drugs is determined by the following:[56]

- Actual acquisition cost (AAC) plus a professional dispensing fee established by the state Medicaid agency;[57] or
- the pharmacies' usual and customary charges to the general public.

States may use any method to set the other drug payment as long as, in the aggregate, state payments for these other drugs are below the levels that would be determined by applying the other drug FUL. The estimated acquisition cost (EAC) is the Medicaid agency's best estimate of the price generally paid by pharmacies and other providers to acquire the drug. CMS allows states flexibility in determining EAC, although many states rely on average wholesale price (AWP) or wholesale acquisition cost (WAC), published prices available from industry compendia.[58] Compendia are reference books or data published by private companies based on data provided by drug manufacturers.[59] Neither AWP nor WAC are necessarily based on actual sales transactions or defined in statute. Thus, both are subject to manufacturers' decisions on what to include or exclude. The AWP is often considered a price for wholesalers to charge retailers.

Maximum Allowable Cost

Most states also often develop their own maximum allowable costs (MACs) for drug pricing. States may select the drugs, including multiple source drugs covered by FULs and other drugs, as well as set the reimbursement amount for drugs subject to MACs. MAC programs enable states to achieve additional drug savings by setting lower reimbursement amounts for more multiple source drugs than for those drugs with FUL prices and using a MAC formula that sets prices lower than FUL amounts.[60] In June 2014, CMS identified 45 states with MACs.[61]

State Payment Formulas

Ingredient Costs

States are not required to use FULs as the basis for reimbursing pharmacies for outpatient drugs dispensed to Medicaid beneficiaries. States must only ensure that federal matching funds are not used to pay drug prices that exceed FULs; there are no other federal rules on how states set drug reimbursement, although payment methodologies are approved by CMS through the state plan amendment (SPA) process. In determining what to pay pharmacies for ingredient costs, states estimate current market prices by using one or several benchmarks to approximate pharmacies' acquisition costs. Historically, AWP was the primary drug pricing benchmark used by state Medicaid to set ingredient reimbursement.

There has been considerable disagreement about the appropriate basis for setting Medicaid multisource drug ingredient reimbursement since statutory changes were passed in DRA.[62] In FY2009, state Medicaid pharmacy directors issued a white paper on AWP alternatives.[63] One of the white paper's suggestions was that CMS develop a single national pricing benchmark based on average drug ingredient acquisition costs. The state pharmacy directors' AWP alternative white paper argued that a single national benchmark would provide better estimates of pharmacy acquisition costs if it were based on actual drug purchases. This approach to drug ingredient price determination, the Medicaid pharmacy directors argued, also would provide greater accuracy and transparency in how drug prices were established. In their AWP alternative white paper, the Medicaid agencies requested that CMS coordinate, develop, and support a national pricing benchmark that could replace AWP. The Department of Health and Human Services Office of Inspector General (OIG) found that AWPs were artificially inflated, which overstated drug EACs and resulted in Medicaid overpayments.[64]

To help states determine ingredient cost reimbursement, the Secretary is required to disclose to states and the general public via a website certain pricing data reported by manufacturers on a monthly basis.[65] The Secretary also is required to disclose the weighted average AMP and an average retail survey price for each multiple source drug.[66] DRA permitted the Secretary to conduct a retail price survey and disclose the survey results to states and the public.[67] CMS initiated a National Average Drug Acquisition Cost (NADAC) survey to identify retail community pharmacy (RCP) drug acquisition costs, or the estimated prices RCPs paid to purchase all Medicaid-covered outpatient drugs.[68] CMS began publishing draft drug acquisition cost data on its website in October 2012 and updates NADAC survey data weekly.[69] CMS also initiated a survey of average retail consumer prices but suspended this retail survey due to funding considerations.[70] State Medicaid directors issued an update on the status of state use of AAC, actual acquisition cost, in setting FFS ingredient reimbursement rates.[71] The Medicaid directors indicated that seven states were using an ACC-based rate in 2014, although only one state was using CMS's NADAC survey data.[72] The other states conducted their own

AAC surveys. States that used an AAC-based methodology generally had increased dispensing fees to offset the potentially lower ingredient payments to pharmacies. Although many states continue to base their Medicaid drug reimbursement on published retail prices, such as AWPs less some percentage or WACs plus some percentage, more states are beginning to transition to AAC (as discussed in the Medicaid director update). Under Medicaid law, states have discretion to use different formulas or percentages to adjust published prices depending on the drug or drug category (i.e., generic versus brand, physician administered, and blood clotting factors).[73]

Dispensing Fees

In addition to a drug ingredient acquisition cost payment, states also pay pharmacies a dispensing fee when they fill a FFS prescription.[74] States determine their dispensing fees, which are limited only insofar as they must be "reasonable."[75] Most dispensing fees generally range from around $1.00 to $3.00 per prescription, but some dispensing fees may reach $10.00 and even more depending on the state methodology and other factors. Dispensing fees may range higher in states that do not use a flat fee.[76] Dispensing fees also often are higher for generics than for single source drugs, and fees can vary by such characteristics as urban or rural location, for profit or non-profit status, and for federally qualified health centers. Some states use tiered dispensing fees, where the rate decreases as a pharmacy's historical annual prescription volume increases. In general, states may set higher dispensing fees to help offset a pharmacy's higher costs for filling certain types of prescriptions or lower profit on reimbursement for ingredients and to encourage generic substitution, where possible.

MEDICAID DRUG REBATES

In 1990, Congress amended the Social Security Act (SSA) to add the Medicaid Drug Rebate (MDR) program to Medicaid law.[77] Under the MDR program, drug manufacturers that want to sell their drugs to state Medicaid agencies must enter into rebate agreements with the Secretary on behalf of states.[78] The MDR agreements require drug manufacturers to provide state Medicaid programs with rebates on drugs purchased for Medicaid beneficiaries to ensure that Medicaid receives the lowest or *best price* for which the manufacturer sold the drug during the previous quarter.[79] In exchange for receiving the best price, Medicaid programs must cover all drugs marketed by those manufacturers with certain exceptions.[80] For instance, drugs provided in hospitals and sometimes in physicians' or dentists' offices, or similar settings are exempt from rebates.[81] Drug manufacturers must pay rebates on prescription drugs provided to Medicaid beneficiaries who receive their care through FFS as well as managed care plans.[82] Drug manufacturers also must pay rebates on some nonprescription, OTC items, such as aspirin, when they are dispensed to a Medicaid beneficiary and covered under the state's Medicaid plan.[83] In 2014, CMS reported there were approximately 610 drug manufacturers participating in the Medicaid drug rebate program.[84] In FY2013, the Medicaid (state and federal) FFS rebates—basic, inflation, and supplemental—were approximately $12.4 billion (see **Table 6**).

Medicaid rebates are shared between the states and the federal government according to state federal medical assistance percentage (FMAP). A state's FMAP determines the rate at which the federal government matches states' Medicaid expenditures.[85] Drug manufacturers compute the drug rebate amount owed each quarter based on utilization information supplied by states. States collect manufacturers' rebates and then subtract (offset) the federal share from the federal matching funds they would receive for Medicaid medical benefits.

For rebates purposes, federal law distinguishes between two major drug categories, single source drugs and multiple source drugs.[86] Multiple source drugs include innovator multiple source drugs—drugs once covered by patents—and non-innovator multiple source drugs—generic drugs and all other drugs, including drugs developed before FDA approval was required and OTC drugs. In addition to the two major drug types, ACA added several additional single source and innovator multiple source drug types that are treated differently for rebates. These drug types include line extensions, clotting (blood) factors, and drugs approved by the FDA for pediatric indications. The basic and additional rebate formulas for these new ACA drug types as well as single source, innovator multiple source, and non-innovator multiple source are summarized in **Table 4**.

Table 4. Medicaid Drug Rebate Formulas

Drug Category	Basic Rebate	Additional Rebate
Single Source	The greater of either 23.1% of AMPa per unit or AMP minus best priceb per unit	Required when prices rise faster than the inflation rates—difference between the products' per unit current AMP and the base period AMP adjusted by CPI-Uc for each quarter since launch.

Drug Category	Basic Rebate	Additional Rebate
Innovator Multiple Source Drugs	The greater of either 23.1% of AMP or AMP minus best price per unit	Required when prices rise faster than the inflation rates—difference between the products' per unit current AMP and the base period AMP adjusted by CPI-U for each quarter since launch.
Line Extension Products[d]	The greater of (1) the basic and additional rebate for the new drug or (2) the product of the line extension drug's AMP and the highest additional rebate for any strength of the original brand drug, and the number of units of each dosage form and strength of the line extension drug.	
Blood Clotting Factors[e]	The greater of 17.1% of AMP per unit or AMP minus best price per unit	Required when prices rise faster than the inflation rates—difference between the products' per unit current AMP and the base period AMP adjusted by CPI-U for each quarter since launch
FDA Approved Pediatric Indication[f]	The greater of 17.1% of AMP per unit or AMP minus best price per unit	Required when prices rise faster than the inflation rates—difference between the product's per unit current AMP and the base period AMP adjusted by CPI-U for each quarter since launch
Non-innovator Multiple Source and Other Drugs	13% of AMP	Not applicable

Source: Congressional Research Service (CRS) review of the SSA § 1927, Payment for Covered Outpatient Drugs, and 42 CFR § 447.502, Definitions.

[a] AMP is the average manufacturer price, or the average U.S. price manufacturers received for their product when sold to retail community pharmacies.

[b] Best price (single source and innovator multiple source) is the drug manufacturer's lowest U.S. price during the reporting period (see the glossary in Appendix E).

[c] CPI-U is the consumer price index for all urban consumers as updated by the U.S. Department of Labor (http://www.bls.gov/cpi/).

[d] A line extension is an oral solid dose (generally a pill or capsule) of a single source or multiple source innovator drug that is a new formulation of an existing drug, such as an extended release formulation (SSA § 1927(c)(2)(C). CMS proposes to use the FDA regulation 21 CFR § 206.3, which defined solid oral dosage form as capsules, tablets, or similar drug products intended for oral use (77 *Federal Register* 5324, February 2, 2012.

[e] Clotting factor drugs receive a separate payment under SSA § 1842(o)(5) and are included on a regularly updated list maintained by the Secretary (SSA § 1927(c)(1)(B)(iii)(II)(aa)).

[f] FDA approved pediatric drugs are those approved for marketing by the FDA for pediatric indications (SSA § 1927(c)(1)(B)(iii)(II)(bb)).

Manufacturer Rebates for Single Source and Innovator Multiple Source Drugs

For single source and innovator multiple source drugs, manufacturers are required to pay state Medicaid programs a basic rebate and, when they raise a drug's price faster than inflation, an additional rebate. As shown in **Table 4**, the basic rebate is determined by comparing each drug's per unit AMP to that drug's per unit best price. The basic rebate is the greater of a specified percentage of AMP or the difference between the AMP and the best price. ACA increased the specified percentage of AMP from 15.1% to 23.1%.[87] Manufacturers owe the additional rebate when a single source or innovator multiple source drugs' per unit AMP is raised faster than the inflation rate.[88] The per unit additional rebate is the amount a drug's quarterly reported AMP exceeds the inflation-adjusted base period AMP. If the per unit quarterly AMP does not exceed the inflation-adjusted base period AMP, then no additional rebate is owed.

To determine the total rebate, a unit rebate amount for each drug—the sum of the basic and additional rebate—is multiplied by the number of units of the drug that were purchased during the quarter, as determined by the Medicaid agency.[89] For line extension products, any version of the original product's base AMP can be used to determine the additional rebate. As displayed in **Table 4**, single source and innovator multiple source pediatric and clotting factor drugs use 17.1% as the percentage to determine the basic rebate amount, but otherwise the rebate calculation, including potential additional rebates, follows the same methodology.

Medicaid law limits manufacturers' total rebate obligation for single source and innovator multiple source drugs for each dosage form and strength to no more than the current period AMP.[90]

Manufacturer Rebates for Non-innovator Multiple Source Drugs

Basic rebates for non-innovator multiple source drugs are equal to 13% of the drug's AMP. Prices offered to other payers are not considered, nor is there an additional rebate for price increases that exceed the inflation rate.

Supplemental Rebates and State Purchasing Pools[91]

In addition to the basic and additional FFS rebates required under federal law, most states negotiate supplemental rebate agreements (SRAs) with prescription drug manufacturers.[92] Although almost all Medicaid SRAs have been for FFS outpatient drugs, in March 2014, three states (Florida, New Hampshire, and Oregon) had submitted SPAs to establish supplemental rebate programs for Medicaid beneficiaries enrolled in managed care plans.

States can negotiate SRAs on their own or by joining with other states to form purchasing pools. In March 2014, 45 states participated in Medicaid outpatient drug SRAs through single- or multiple-state purchasing pools. States that participate in multi-state purchasing pools are able to combine their purchasing power with that of other states to negotiate greater supplemental rebates and other price concessions from manufacturers. Some states also have established intra-state pools that negotiate drug prices for Medicaid drugs as well as for drugs dispensed through other state agencies such as employee health and local government programs. Generally, states must submit SPAs to CMS outlining their SRA arrangements.[93]

Managed Care Rebates

Prior to ACA, drug manufacturers were not required to pay rebates on drugs purchased for Medicaid beneficiaries by managed care plans. To collect rebates for managed care beneficiaries, states excluded or *carved out* drug benefits from capitation agreements, then provided drug benefits under FFS or contracted with other entities, such as PBM companies, to provide drug benefits.[94] Beginning in January 2010, prescription drug manufacturers were required under ACA to pay rebates the same rebates that were required under FFS on drugs provided to Medicaid beneficiaries enrolled in managed care plans.[95] Since ACA became law, some states have *carved in* prescription drug benefits to their managed care contracts, so that drugs are covered under these contracts. Managed care rebates are paid to states and shared with the federal government following the same formulas as FFS rebates. As shown in **Table 5**, Medicaid managed care rebates increased substantially since 2011.

Table 5. Total Medicaid Managed Care Drug Rebates FY2011-FY2013

Fiscal Year	Drug Rebates[a] Basic and Additional Rebates (in $ millions)	Supplemental Rebates (in $ millions)	All Rebates (in $ millions)
2011	$932.76	$0	$932.76
2012	$2,565.54	$0.72	$2,566.26
2013	$4,653.42	$92.69	$4,746.11

Source: CRS analysis of Medicaid Statement of Expenditures for the Medical Assistance Program (CMS Form 64 report).

a. The rebates include federal and state shares. State supplemental rebates are not required under federal law. States negotiate supplemental rebates with drug wholesalers and manufacturers, but rebates are shared according to FMAP rates between states and the federal government.

National and State FY2013 FFS Drug Expenditures and Rebates

Table 6 displays FY2013 Medicaid FFS outpatient drug expenditures and total rebates for each state and all states. In FY2013, total Medicaid FFS outpatient prescription drug expenditures, before rebates, were about $19.8 billion (federal and state shares, Table 6). Also in FY2013, states reported collecting approximately $12.4 billion in FFS drug rebates from drug manufacturers which includes approximately $726 million in supplemental rebates not required under federal Medicaid law (Table 6) and $11.7 billion in required rebates. Net FY2013 Medicaid drug expenditures (after all rebates) were approximately $7.4 billion (Table 7).

The Table 6 data may overstate Medicaid FFS rebates. ACA increased the basic rebate percentage and extended manufacturers' additional rebate obligations to line extensions. These ACA changes were retroactive to January 1, 2010. Implementation and accounting for the ACA rebate changes may have lagged behind so that states reported rebates attributable to FY2010-FY2012 utilization in the FY2013 CMS financial reports. In addition, beginning in 2010 with the added authority for states to collect rebates on drugs purchased for full-risk Medicaid managed care beneficiaries; there may have been delays in identifying transactions that were subject to the managed care rebate.[96]

Table 6. Medicaid FFS Drug Expenditures and Rebates (by State for FY2013)

State	Total FFS Drug Expendituresa (in $ millions)	All FFS Rebates Collectedb (in $ millions)	Net FFS Drug Expendituresc (in $ millions)
Alabama	$534.0	$222.6	$311.4
Alaska	$63.0	$35.6	$27.5
Arizona	$7.8	$2.5	$5.3
Arkansas	$293.6	$126.0	$167.5
California	$2,504.2	$1,633.3	$870.9
Colorado	$344.9	$168.2	$176.7
Connecticut	$692.0	$362.7	$329.2
Delaware	$174.0	$103.2	$70.8
District of Columbia	$101.8	$37.1	$64.8
Florida	$1,336.7	$703.9	$632.8
Georgia	$529.8	$303.2	$226.7
Hawaii	$0.0	$0.2	($0.2)
Idaho	$129.8	$69.4	$60.4
Illinois	$956.9	$547.6	$409.3
Indiana	$761.7	$389.9	$371.8
Iowa	$253.1	$139.7	$113.4
Kansas	$42.8	$55.2	($12.4)
Kentucky	$62.3	$28.3	$33.9
Louisiana	$584.4	$384.0	$200.4
Maine	$197.9	$132.5	$65.4
Maryland	$341.2	$193.0	$148.3
Massachusetts	$486.7	$229.4	$257.3
Michigan	$643.8	$352.9	$290.9
Minnesota	$223.3	$103.5	$119.8
Mississippi	$262.8	$131.4	$131.5
Missouri	$1,061.9	$373.3	$688.6
Montana	$78.1	$43.9	$34.2
Nebraska	$160.4	$79.5	$80.8
Nevada	$131.9	$71.3	$60.5
New Hampshire	$95.3	$58.5	$36.8
New Jersey	$132.8	$34.9	$97.9
New Mexico	$20.3	$113.9	($93.5)
New York	$750.8	$2,032.0	($1,281.2)
North Carolina	$1,237.7	$456.1	$781.7
North Dakota	$41.9	$18.1	$23.9
Ohio	$473.1	$268.3	$204.8

Table 6. (Continued)

State	Total FFS Drug Expendituresa (in $ millions)	All FFS Rebates Collectedb (in $ millions)	Net FFS Drug Expendituresc (in $ millions)
Oklahoma	$478.7	$169.2	$309.5
Oregon	$120.3	$42.7	$77.6
Pennsylvania	$176.4	$199.6	($23.2)
Rhode Island	$17.9	$15.6	$2.3
South Carolina	$204.5	$123.9	$80.6
South Dakota	$52.2	$22.4	$29.8
Tennessee	$776.1	$455.0	$321.2
Texas	$719.4	$412.6	$306.9
Utah	$121.2	$69.0	$52.2
Vermont	$3.4	$66.5	($63.2)
Virginia	$134.4	$97.8	$36.6
Washington	$215.1	$163.3	$51.7
West Virginia	$312.9	$199.5	$113.4
Wisconsin	$697.3	$357.4	$339.9
Wyoming	$38.6	$18.6	$20.0
National Total	$19,781.3	$12,418.2	$7,363.2

Source: Congressional Research Service (CRS) analysis of CMS Financial Management Reports (CMS Form 64 data).

[a] Drug expenditures are shown as reported by each state.

[b] Includes federal and state shares for national rebates as well as state sidebar agreements. Net expenditures are drug expenditures less federal and state rebates.

[c] Six states reported net FFS prescription drug expenditures that were less than total rebate collections: Hawaii, Kansas, New Mexico, New York, Pennsylvania, and Vermont. The higher rebate collections were probably due to lags in reporting rebates for previous periods, such as the increased rebates authorized by ACA.

Table 7 displays the total amount of SRA rebates collected by states for FY1997-FY2013. In FY2013, 42 states collected a total of $726 million in supplemental FFS rebates ($403 million federal share).[97] In FY2013, California accounted for 23% of the reported supplemental rebates (federal and state shares).

Table 7. Total Medicaid FFS *Supplemental* Drug Rebates FY1997-FY2013

Fiscal Year	Fee-for-Service Supplemental Rebates (in $ millions)a	Fee-for-Service Supplemental Rebate Annual % Change
1997	$48	—
1998	$54	13.0%
1999	$78	44.7%
2000	$222	184.9%
2001	$222	-0.3%
2002	$304	37.2%
2003	$471	54.9%
2004	$851	80.6%
2005	$1,307	53.6%
2006	$1,533	17.3%
2007	$995	-35.1%
2008	$894	-10.1%
2009	$948	6.0%
2010	$1,041	9.8%
2011	$928	10.8%
2012	$972	4.7%
2013	$726	-25.3%

Source: CRS analysis of Medicaid Statement of Expenditures for the Medical Assistance Program (CMS Form 64 report).

[a] Rebates include federal and state shares. Supplemental rebates are not required under federal law. States negotiate supplemental rebates with drug wholesalers and manufacturers, but rebates are shared according to federal medical assistance percentage (FMAP) rates between states and the federal government.

NATIONAL FFS DRUG EXPENDITURE TRENDS

Some data seem to suggest that Medicaid FFS drug expenditures have decreased dramatically since FY2006, but net spending changes are attributable at least in part to policy changes that have shifted drug spending from Medicaid to Medicare, increased rebates, and shifted drug coverage from FFS to managed care plans. This section discusses recent Medicaid FFS drug expenditures and patterns.

Table 8. Medicaid FFS Benefit and Prescription Drug Expenditures FY1997-FY2013

Fiscal Year	Total FFS Benefit Expendituresa (in $ billions)	FFS Benefit Expenditure Annual % Change	FFS Drug Expendituresb (in $ billions)	FFS Drug Expenditure Annual % Change
1997	$160.0	—	$10.2	—
1998	$168.6	5.1%	$11.7	13.1%
1999	$180.0	6.3%	$13.7	14.7%
2000	$195.2	7.8%	$16.6	17.3%
2001	$215.8	9.6%	$19.7	15.9%
2002	$245.7	12.2%	$23.4	15.8%
2003	$261.8	6.1%	$26.6	12.0%
2004	$280.8	6.8%	$30.4	12.5%
2005	$299.7	6.3%	$30.7	0.1%
2006	$298.1	-0.5%	$23.1	-32.9%
2007	$315.0	5.4%	$21.9	-5.3%
2008	$333.1	5.4%	$22.3	1.5%
2009	$359.2	7.3%	$23.4	4.9%
2010	$382.3	6.1%	$19.7	-19.1%
2011	$406.4	5.2%	$23.1	14.7%
2012	$407.1	0.2%	$18.4	-25.3%
2013	$431.1	5.6%	$16.2	-13.6%

Source: CRS analysis of CMS Form 64 data and Financial Management Report.

[a] Excludes administrative costs and territory medical assistance, including prescription drug expenditures.

[b] Excludes prescription drugs paid through managed care capitation agreements, obtained directly from physicians, or bundled in claims for other services, such as institutional care and home health care. Excludes territory prescription drug expenditures. National federal and state supplemental rebates were subtracted from drug expenditures, but rebates attributable to drugs dispensed under managed care capitation agreements were excluded. Medicaid outpatient prescription drug expenditures include state and federal payments under SSA § 1935(c)(1), Phased-down State Contribution (PSC, *Clawback*). Under § 1935(c)(1), beginning January 1, 2006, drug costs for dual eligibles were assumed by Medicare Part D, although a maintenance of effort provision required states to pay a percentage of those costs. In 2006, states paid 90% of dual eligible drug costs; this percentage was phased-down to 75% in FY2015 and subsequent fiscal years. CMS estimated that total FY2013 state clawback payments were approximately $8.8 billion.

In FY1997, states reported total FFS outpatient prescription drug expenditures, net of all rebates—federal and state shares—of about $10.2 billion, or 6.3% of total program spending. In FY2005, total FFS outpatient prescription drug expenditures, net of all rebates—federal and state shares—were $30.7 billion, accounting for about 10.2% of Medicaid benefit expenditures.[98] By FY2013, net Medicaid FFS outpatient drug expenditures had decreased to about $16.2 billion and accounted for less than 4% of benefit expenditures. Table 8 displays a summary of Medicaid benefit and outpatient prescription drug expenditures for FY1997-FY2013.

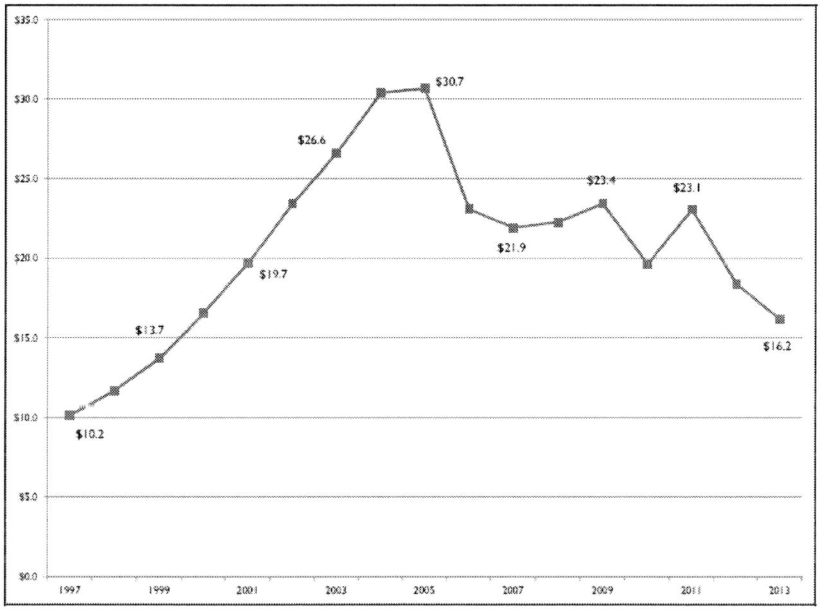

Source: CRS analysis of CMS Medicaid Financial Management Reports, (CMS Form-64).

Notes: CMS Form-64 data were adjusted to exclude territory drug expenditures. CMS medical and drug expenditures exclude administration and drug expenditures that were included in capitated managed care contracts. Drug expenditure data are net of federal and state rebates but include phased-down state contribution payments for FY2006-FY2013. These CMS Form-64 data include both federal and state shares.

Figure 1. Net Medicaid FFS Prescription Drug Expenditures; FY1997-FY2013 (in $billions).

The variation in prescription drug expenditures and year-to-year percentage changes shown in **Table 8** were attributable to a number of factors. Some of these factors are trends affecting the prescription drug industry and health care markets in general, such as the expiration of prescription drug patents sometimes called the *patent-cliff* and increasing managed care enrollment.[99] Other policy changes attributable to federal law may be more important than industry trends in explaining Medicaid prescription drug expenditure changes. The amendments to Medicaid drug law helped to reduce outpatient Medicaid prescription drug expenditures.[100] **Figure 1** displays the recent history of Medicaid FFS outpatient prescription drug expenditures.

There are several changes shown in Figure 1 that coincide with implementation of major legislative changes. Prior to MMA, drug expenditures were steadily increasing, rising from approximately $10.2 billion in 1997 to about $30.7 billion in 2005, even though federal and state (but particularly state) rebates also were increasing. In 2006, there was a substantial decrease (of approximately $7.6 billion) in Medicaid drug expenditures to $23.1 billion when dual eligible drug expenditures were moved to Medicare Part D.[101]

In 2010, adjusted Medicaid drug expenditures dipped again to $19.7 billion. This change was in part attributable to the fiscal relief provided to states in the form of ARRA's temporary FMAP increase, which reduced state drug expenditures because it was applied to states' phased-down state contribution (PSC) payments.[102, 103] PSC payments declined from $7.8 in FY2009 to $3.8 billion in FY2010. The PSC decrease shifted a portion of prescription drug costs from state and federal Medicaid matching funds to federal economic recovery funding, thus reducing federal and state Medicaid drug expenditures. Although this also increased federal funding, it shifted that funding from Medicaid to another source. Net FFS drug expenditures returned to approximately the FY2009 level in FY2011 after deducting all rebates but adding in the PSC amount that states would have paid for dual eligible drug expenditures to make comparison with earlier periods consistent.

In FY2011, the increased rebate percentages and other ACA changes were just beginning to take effect. These changes boosted federal and state rebates, but drug expenditures increased considerably to $23.1 billion from $19.7 billion in FY2010. The FY2011 increase was probably attributable to reporting delays of the ACA's rebate increases. In FY2012 and FY2013, Medicaid outpatient drug expenditures (after rebates and other adjustments) were substantially reduced, falling from about $23.1 billion in FY2011 to about $18.4 billion in FY2012 and $16.2 billion in FY2013. The FY2012 and

FY2013 decreases were somewhat due to modest ACA rebate increases and the rapid movement of Medicaid beneficiaries to managed care coverage that included prescription drugs. As previously discussed, these changes did not reduce prescription drug expenditures, but shifted drug expenditures to other reports.

However, looking at state Medicaid drug utilization reports, as shown in Table 9, estimated (unadjusted, before all rebates and PSC) total Medicaid expenditures for FFS and managed care were higher and consistent with historic drug spending patterns.

Table 9. Estimated Total Medicaid FFS and Managed Care Drug Expenditures FY2010-FY2013 (in $billions)

Fiscal Year	FFS	Managed Care	Totala
2010	$29.54	$3.14	$32.68
2011	$29.94	$7.56	$37.50
2012	$23.39	$18.38	$41.77
2013	$20.80	$15.98	$36.77

Source: CRS analysis of Medicaid drug utilization reports, submitted by each state.

a. These expenditure data are unadjusted, meaning they are before rebates and other payments, such as Phased-down State Contribution (PSCs).

Although Medicaid drug expenditures for both managed care and FFS appear to be close to their historic levels, expenditures did decline between FY2012 and FY2013 in similar ways for both managed care and FFS drug spending. The decrease could be attributable to different data sources as well as the previously mentioned reporting lags and the patent cliff.

Additional data from Medicaid financial reports can provide insight into how Medicaid FFS drug expenditures only have changed over time (not managed care). It is possible to estimate a new FFS drug expenditure by aggregating drug expenditures and rebates and by adjusting for the Medicaid drug expenditures that were moved to Medicare Part D. The net FFS drug expenditure data can then be compared with earlier periods (before 2006) to help identify changes. As shown in **Table 10**, the net FFS drug spending decrease between FY2012 and FY2013 was primarily due to decreased prescription drug expenditures, rather than increased rebate collections.

Table 10. Adjusted Medicaid FFS Prescription Drug Expenditures FY1997-FY2013 (in $ billions)

Fiscal Year	FFS Drug Expenditures	State & Federal FFS Rebates	Phased-down State Contribution (*Clawback*)	Net FFS Drug Expendituresa
1997	$12.41	$2.26	$0	$10.15
1998	$14.16	$2.47	$0	$11.69
1999	$17.05	$3.34	$0	$13.71
2000	$20.55	$3.98	$0	$16.57
2001	$24.66	$4.95	$0	$19.71
2002	$29.34	$5.92	$0	$23.42
2003	$33.91	$7.31	$0	$26.60
2004	$40.07	$9.65	$0	$30.41
2005	$43.08	$12.41	$0	$30.67
2006	$28.22	$11.56	$6.42	$23.08
2007	$22.29	$7.33	$6.97	$21.93
2008	$23.60	$8.39	$7.06	$22.27
2009	$25.37	$9.72	$7.77	$23.42
2010	$27.34	$11.43	$3.76	$19.66
2011	$29.79	$14.16	$7.42	$23.06
2012	$23.25	$13.38	$8.53	$18.40
2013	$19.78	$12.42	$8.83	$16.20

Source: CRS analysis of Medicaid Statement of Expenditures for the Medical Assistance Program (CMS Form 64 report). Phased-down State Contribution (PSC) data provided by CMS.

Notes: Data include state and federal drug expenditures but exclude U.S. territories.

[a] *Total net FFS drug expenditures* as shown the Table's last column were determined from the following: drug expenditures (column 2), minus rebates (column 3), plus PSC (column 4).

FY2012 and FY2013 FFS drug expenditures fell by 20% and 12% respectively from the previous year. The FY2012 and FY2013 decreases in Medicaid FFS drug expenditures may have been caused by several factors, including the rapid growth of Medicaid managed care enrollment that included prescription drug coverage.

In FY2012 and FY2013, total Medicaid FFS drug rebate collections also decreased. The decrease in FFS drug rebates was due to reduced FFS drug expenditures—fewer drugs purchased translates to lower rebate collections.

FFS Drug Expenditures by Eligibility Group

This section reviews drug expenditure patterns among the major Medicaid eligibility groups in FY2005 and FY2010 (the latest year data were available). Traditionally, the majority of Medicaid expenditures have been concentrated among the elderly and disabled eligibility groups, which account for the fewest beneficiaries. In contrast, the children and family eligibility groups, typically account for more individuals and lower expenditures.

Table 11. Average Medicaid FFS Drug Expenditures and Beneficiaries Who Received Drugs by Basis of Eligibility FY2005 and FY2010

	Percentage of Medicaid Beneficiaries with Drug Expenditures		Average Medicaid Drug Spending per Beneficiary with Drug Expenditures	
Basis of Eligibility (BOE)	FY2005	FY2010	FY2005	FY2010
Aged	71%	45%	$2,943	$451
Blind or Disabled	75%	61%	$3,793	$2,692
Child	51%	40%	$323	$379
Adults	47%	48%	$627	$679
Foster Care Children	58%	59%	$1,141	$1,363
Breast and Cervical Cancer Act (BCCA) Women	73%	74%	$2,121	$2,620
Total	49%	45%	$1,509	$926

Source: CRS analysis of CMS Medicaid Statistical Information System (MSIS) State Summary Datamart FY2005 and FY2010 data. Data for all states and the District of Columbia were included for both FY2005 and FY2010.

Notes: MSIS data exclude Medicaid drug rebates and drugs included in claims for other services, such as institutional care. FY2005 data exclude reimbursement to physicians for drugs provided in their offices, but FY2010 data include some of these drugs. These MSIS data are only for FFS drug expenditures. They exclude prescription drugs paid through managed care capitation agreements, obtained directly from physicians, or bundled in claims for other services, such as institutional care and home health care.

The drug expenditure data by basis of eligibility (BOE) show how drug utilization patterns have changed since FY2005 with more drug spending for children and adults and less was for the aged and disabled eligibility groups. These changes were probably mostly due to the movement of drug coverage for beneficiaries who were dually eligible for both Medicare and Medicaid from Medicaid to Medicare Part D, the outpatient prescription drug benefit that began January 1, 2006. Table 11 displays FFS drug use and average payments by BOE.

As shown in **Table 11**, in FY2005, about 71% of Medicaid beneficiaries who were eligible because they were elderly had drug expenditures and Medicaid paid on average about $2,943 annually for their drugs. By FY2010, about 45% of Medicaid beneficiaries who were eligible because they were elderly had prescription drug expenditures, but Medicaid paid only about $451 annually for their drugs. This dramatic decrease in the number of elderly using drugs and the amount of expenditures for those drugs is mostly attributable to the MMA change that shifted outpatient drug coverage for dual eligibles, a group that typically has high drug utilization and costs, to Medicare Part D. However, even though drug costs for dual eligibles were shifted to Medicare Part D, states continued to pay the vast majority of these costs through the phased-down state contribution. Thus, the data shown in **Table 11** include dual eligibles' outpatient prescription drug costs in FY2005 but do not include these expenditures in FY2010.[104] **Table 11** also shows that children had the lowest average spending and that blind or disabled enrollees had the highest. Among blind or disabled enrollees with prescription drug spending, the average amount was about $3,793 in FY2005 but had declined to about $2,692 in FY2010. For children with prescription drug spending, the average annual amount paid for drugs was about $323 in FY2005 and $379 in FY2010.

Even though these data exclude expenditures for dual eligible and Medicaid beneficiaries enrolled in Medicaid managed care plans, they provide a glimpse of the FFS spending among different eligibility groups.[105] Among all Medicaid beneficiaries who were dispensed drugs in FY2005, the average annual Medicaid prescription drug spending was about $1,509. By FY2010, average per beneficiary annual expenditures had declined to about $926. Again, this decrease probably was due to the following combination of factors: the movement of dual eligible drug coverage from Medicaid to Medicare Part D, other Medicaid drug pricing changes, the increased availability of a number of commonly prescribed drugs as generic rather than brand-name drugs, and other trends affecting prescription drugs.

Number and Cost of Medicaid FFS Prescriptions

Table 12 displays a summary of the number of prescriptions filled for different drug types— single source, innovator, and non-innovator multiple source drugs—and the total amount states reported reimbursing providers for these drugs. The mix of drugs prescribed by state Medicaid programs affects FFS drug expenditures, with single source drugs representing a higher cost than both innovator and non-innovator multiple source drugs. As Table 12 shows, Medicaid agencies reported processing more than 323.5 million prescription claims in FY2012 and the national average Medicaid FFS payment was about $72.[106]

Table 12. Medicaid FFS Claims, Payment, and Average Payment by Drug Category FY2011-FY2012

	FY2011			FY2012		
Drug Category	Claims (in millions)	Payment[a] (in $ billions)	Average Payment[b]	Claims (in millions)	Payment[a] (in $ billions)	Average Payment[b]
Single Source	75.5	19.1	$253	51.1	14.4	$282
Innovator Multiple Source	32.3	4.3	$134	29.7	4.4	$149
Non-innovator Multiple Source (generic)	281.2	5.0	$18	242.7	4.4	$18
National Total	388.9	28.4	$73	323.5	23.2	$72

Source: CRS analysis of CMS's Medicaid FFS prescription drug utilization review (DUR) reports submitted by each state.

Notes: States are required to submit annual Medicaid DUR survey reports, SSA § 1927(g)(3)(D). Arizona has a statewide SSA § 1115 Medicaid managed care waiver. Under the waiver most services are provided under capitation agreements. Arizona did not report FFS drug utilization data in FY2011 and FY2012. In addition, Hawaii has a statewide § 1115 Medicaid managed care waiver where most beneficiaries are enrolled in managed care. Hawaii also reports minimal FFS drug utilization data. A number of other states use § 1115 waivers to provide services to some Medicaid beneficiaries. All states have some managed care contracts that include drug benefit coverage. Managed care drug expenditure analysis is beyond the scope of this report. FY2011 data for the District of Columbia and Louisiana were unavailable.

[a] Payments are prior to all rebates.

[b] Average payment is calculated by dividing the payments by the number of claims.

The national data shown in Table 12 are available for each state in Appendix A and Appendix B, which show that in FY2012 average state per prescription payment for all drug categories, before rebates, ranged from a high of about $131 in Colorado to a low of about $35 in Nevada.[107] Table 12 shows that the FY2012 average payment for single source prescription claims was $282 and about $18 for each generic prescription.

Table 13. Medicaid FFS Drug Claims, by Drug Category FY2011-FY2012

	FY2011		FY2012	
Drug Category	FFS Drug Claims (in millions)	% of Total	FFS Drug Claims (in millions)	% of Total
Single Source	75.5	19.4%	51.1	15.8%
Innovator Multiple Source	32.3	8.3%	29.7	9.2%
Non-innovator Multiple Source	281.2	72.3%	242.7	75.0%
National Total	388.9	100.0%	323.5	100.0%

Source: CRS analysis of CMS's Medicaid FFS prescription DUR reports submitted by each state.

Notes: States are required to submit annual Medicaid DUR survey reports, SSA § 1927(g)(3)(D). Arizona has a statewide SSA § 1115 Medicaid managed care waiver. Under the waiver most services are provided under capitation agreements. Arizona did not report FFS drug utilization data in FY2011 and FY2012. In addition, Hawaii has a statewide § 1115 Medicaid managed care waiver where most beneficiaries are enrolled in managed care. Hawaii also reports minimal FFS drug utilization data. A number of other states use § 1115 waivers to provide services to some Medicaid beneficiaries. All states have some managed care contracts that include drug benefit coverage. Managed care drug payment analysis is beyond the scope of this report. FY2011 data for DC and LA were unavailable.

Similar to Table 12, Table 13 displays the number of Medicaid FFS drug claims for FY2011 and FY2012, but also shows the percentage of claims of the total that were attributable to each drug category. From FY2011 to FY2012 the percentage of claims attributable to single source products declined from about 19% to about 16% and the percentage of non-innovator multiple source prescription claims increased from about 72% to 75%. During that period (FY2011-FY2012), the overall total volume of FFS claims declined by approximately 17% from about 389 million to 324 million claims.[108] The decline in the overall volume of FFS prescriptions is probably due to states rapidly shifting beneficiaries into managed care plans that provide prescription drug coverage under their capitated rates, rather than through carved out FFS arrangements. The increase in the percentage of claims for generic versus brand products is probably due to the patent cliff.

Also similar to Table 12, Table 14 displays FY2011 and FY2012 Medicaid FFS drug expenditures by drug category drug expenditures, but also shows the percentage of total annual FFS drug expenditures attributable to the different drug categories. As shown in Table 14, national total Medicaid FFS drug expenditures, before rebates, decreased by about 18% from $28.4 billion to about $23.2 billion from FY2011 to FY2012. However, expenditures for single source Medicaid FFS drugs declined, but expenditures for multiple source non-innovator drugs increased.

Table 14. Medicaid FFS Drug Expenditures, by Drug Category FY2011-FY2012

	FY2011		FY2012	
Drug Category	**Total FFS Drug Expenditures[a] (in $ billion)**	**% of Total**	**Total FFS Drug Expenditures (in $ billion)**	**% of Total**
Single Source	$19.1	67.2%	$14.4	62.1%
Innovator Multiple Source	$4.3	15.2%	$4.4	19.1%
Non-innovator Multiple Source	$5.0	17.5%	$4.4	18.8%
National Total	$28.4	100.0%	$23.2	100.0%

Source: CRS analysis of CMS's Medicaid FFS prescription DUR reports submitted by each state.

Notes: States are required to submit annual Medicaid DUR survey reports, SSA § 1927 (g) (3) (D). Arizona has a statewide SSA § 1115 Medicaid managed care waiver. Under the waiver, most services are provided under capitation agreements. Arizona did not report FFS drug utilization data in FY2011 and FY2012. In addition, Hawaii has a statewide § 1115 Medicaid managed care waiver under which most beneficiaries are enrolled in managed care. Hawaii also reports minimal FFS drug utilization data. A number of other states use § 1115 waivers to provide services to some Medicaid beneficiaries. All states have some managed care contracts that include drug benefit coverage. Managed care drug payment analysis is beyond the scope of this report. FY2011 data for the District of Columbia and Louisiana were unavailable.

[a] Payments are prior to all rebates.

Table 13 and **Table 14** together show that single source drug expenditures represent the majority of Medicaid FFS drug expenditures, accounting for more than 60% of Medicaid FFS drug spending in both FY2011 and FY2012, even though single source drugs accounted for less than 20% of total drug claims in those years. These data are before rebates. If rebates were deducted, the differences between the percentage of expenditures for single source and multiple source drugs might be closer because single source drug rebates are considerably more than rebates for multiple source drugs. CBO estimated that Medicaid's 2010 basic and additional rebate on single source drugs averaged 57% of manufacturers' average prices.[109]

POLICIES TO CONTROL PROGRAM DRUG EXPENDITURES AND UTILIZATION

Medicaid law permits states to use other techniques in addition to FULs and formularies to help monitor and control overall drug expenditures and utilization. Some techniques to control drug spending involve encouraging the use of lower cost, but generically or therapeutically equivalent products, and other techniques involve establishing limits that encourage appropriate utilization. The discussion in this section is primarily applicable to the administration of Medicaid FFS drug benefits, but policies to help control drug spending are widely used by all insurers that provide prescription drug coverage, including the private sector and managed care plans under contract to state Medicaid programs.

All states use all or most of these policies in some form, although there is considerable variation in the degree to which states use these policies. For instance, all states have prior authorization, but many states only require prior authorization for certain drugs. In addition, some states allow managed care plans to establish their own prior authorization procedures and policies.[110]

One common cost and utilization process is prior authorization and the use of preferred drug lists (PDLs). PDLs identify pharmaceutical products that have been approved in advance by a committee because they were determined to be clinically effective, but lower cost than other alternative products.[111] Providers may readily prescribe these products to Medicaid beneficiaries.[112] Other non-PDL drugs also are covered but may only be available when they are specifically requested and approved or authorized by the Medicaid agency. Non-PDL drugs must be prior authorized or approved. When providers want to prescribe non-PDL drugs to beneficiaries, the providers (either the physician or the pharmacist) must request permission from the state Medicaid program or the program's contractor to dispense the drug.

States may establish prior authorization programs under Medicaid for all drugs or for certain classes of drugs, as long as these programs meet the following two criteria:

1) they must respond within 24 hours to a request for approval, and
2) they must dispense at least a 72-hour supply of a covered drug in emergency situations without prior authorization.

States also may restrict the quantity of prescription drugs available to beneficiaries. Such prescribing and dispensing limits are common. The most prevalent constraint is on the drug quantity that may be dispensed for each prescription. A number of states routinely limit the amount of certain drugs dispensed to a 30-day to 34-day supply. In addition, states also sometimes limit the number of prescriptions a beneficiary can have without special approval, particularly for single source products. In 2010, 14 states limited the total number of prescriptions (single and multiple source) per beneficiary and four states capped the monthly number of prescriptions per beneficiary. The remaining 32 states, which accounted for about 40% of Medicaid's 2010 FFS drug expenditures, did not cap the number of monthly prescriptions.[113]

Drug Use Review

All states use policies to control the use of outpatient prescription drugs, and all have programs in place to assess the quality of their pharmaceutical programs. OBRA1990 required states to establish drug use review (DUR) programs by January 1993 and provided temporary enhanced federal matching payment for DUR program start-up costs.[114] In general, DUR programs are aimed at both improving the quality of pharmaceutical care and assisting in cost containment.[115] Selected major DUR program design features include the following: pharmacists and physicians education in identification of fraud, abuse, gross overuse, or inappropriate or medically unnecessary care; enhanced communication between pharmacists and beneficiaries; and educational outreach for pharmacists, physicians, and beneficiaries; and pharmacy counseling.

States are required to modify their Medicaid state plans to include both prospective and retrospective drug review. Prospective review is provided to beneficiaries before drugs are dispensed, whereas retrospective review is conducted after the sale on drug claims and other data using information technology.[116]

States also are required to establish DUR boards that include appropriate health care professionals with knowledge and expertise in outpatient prescription drug prescribing, dispensing, monitoring, DUR, education, intervention, and medical quality assurance. DUR boards must include physicians and pharmacists. States are required to submit an annual DUR report to the Secretary that includes information on DUR board activity as well as on state outpatient prescription drug utilization. CMS is required to evaluate the effectiveness of each state's DUR program.[117] Most state DUR programs are operated by vendors, and these vendors also often overlap with state fiscal agents.[118] Based on state DUR reports, the national average generic prescribing rate was about 74% in FY2011 and about 76% in FY2012. Table D-1 displays a summary of state generic prescribing rates for FY2011 and FY2012.

Medicaid Prescription Drug Beneficiary Cost-Sharing Requirements

In addition to prior authorization and utilization review, many state Medicaid programs impose beneficiary cost-sharing to help control drug use and spending. Federal Medicaid law permits states to require beneficiaries to pay out of pocket costs to encourage the most cost-effective prescription drug use.[119] To encourage the use of lower-cost drugs, states may establish different generic versus brand-name copayments for drugs included on a PDL. For people with incomes above 150% of FPL, copayments for non-preferred drugs may be as high as 20% of what Medicaid paid for the drug's ingredients. For people with income at or below 150% of FPL, copayments are limited to nominal amounts. State Medicaid programs must specify which drugs are preferred or non-preferred. States also have the option to establish different copayments for mail-order drugs than for those sold in pharmacies.

DRA amended the SSA to permit increased Medicaid prescription drug cost-sharing for Medicaid beneficiaries. Prior to DRA, most FFS cost-sharing was limited to "nominal" copayments.[120] DRA established two additional cost-sharing options for states.[121] The first option allows states to establish cost-sharing that exceeds nominal amounts and to vary the cost-sharing among beneficiary classes and groups or by service types. The second option, which applies specifically to outpatient prescription drugs, allows states to require beneficiaries to pay higher copayments for state-identified non-preferred drugs and no, or reduced, copayments for preferred drugs. Table 15 displays the maximum copayments states may charge for preferred and non-preferred drugs.

Table 15. Prescription Drug Maximum Allowable Cost-Sharing (preferred and non-preferred drugs)

	Income Level	
Drug Category	Less than or Equal to 150% of FPL	Greater than 150% of FPL
Preferred drug	$4.00	$4.00
Non-preferred drugs	$8.00	Up to 20% of a drug's Medicaid cost

Source: 42 CFR § 447.53, Cost-Sharing for Drugs.

The two cost-sharing options come with additional limitations. Besides the specifically exempted groups, cost-sharing cannot exceed 10% of the cost of the item or service for individuals with income between 100% of FPL and 150% of FPL and 20% of the cost of the item or service for individuals with an income over 150% of FPL. Annual aggregate cost-sharing for all Medicaid benefits cannot exceed 5% of family income. Medicaid beneficiaries can be denied services for non-payment of alternative cost-sharing.

Other Cost-Containment Strategies

Some states manage drug costs through the use of PBMs. Many private insurers, including those that provide coverage to federal employees under the Federal Employees Health Benefits Program (FEHBP), contract with PBMs for drug benefits management and claims payment.[122] PBMs enable insurers to obtain discounts for pharmaceuticals that would not otherwise be available to single insurers because the PBMs administer multiple insurers' covered populations. In addition, PBMs sometimes provide administrative services intended to improve quality and control costs, such as retail pharmacy network development, mail-order pharmacy operation, formulary development, manufacturer rebate negotiation, and prescription checks for adverse drug interactions.[123] PBMs administer a substantial portion of private health insurance prescription drug benefits and are employed by some states to administer Medicaid drug benefits, often through managed care arrangements.

SELECTED MEDICAID PRESCRIPTION DRUG LAWS

The Medicaid rebate program was authorized by Omnibus Budget Reconciliation Act of 1990 (OBRA90, P.L. 101-508), then amended in 1992 by the Veterans Health Care Act of 1992 (P.L. 102-585). After 1992, there were few federal statutory changes to Medicaid prescription drug pricing until 2003, when the Medicare Prescription Drug Improvement and Modernization Act of 2003 (MMA, P.L. 108-173) was passed. MMA was the first of five laws that reshaped Medicaid drug pricing policy. These changes had a number of goals, such as increasing the amount of rebates collected by states and the federal government and strengthening the ability of states and federal policy makers to monitor and enforce compliance. A number of recent changes were made to improve or revise earlier amendments that did not achieve the desired results.

Prescription drug policies are complicated in part because it is hard to isolate the effects of changes in a dynamic market with many private purchasers and sellers. For Medicaid, prescription drug rebates and pricing changes are further complicated because each state has some discretion in how changes are implemented and enforced. This section provides a discussion of major legislative changes to Medicaid prescription drug pricing and rebates. Table 16 displays a summary of major laws with Medicaid drug pricing provisions.

Table 16. Summary of Selected Major Laws Affecting Medicaid Prescription Drugs

Public Law	**Summary of Major Outpatient Prescription Drug Provisions**
Omnibus Budget Reconciliation Act of 1990 (OBRA90, P.L. 101-508)	• Required drug manufacturers to give states and federal government best price rebates for outpatient prescription drugs.
Veterans Health Care Act of 1992 (VHCA, P.L. 102-585)	• Revised Medicaid's best price requirements to exclude nominal price sales to certain Veterans Health Administration (VHA), Department of Defense (DOD), and Public Health Service (PHS) providers.

Public Law	Summary of Major Outpatient Prescription Drug Provisions
Omnibus Budget Reconciliation Act of 1993 (OBRA93, P.L. 103-66)	• Established formulary standards for states to use to limit drug coverage.
Medicare Prescription Drug Improvement and Modernization Act of 2003 (MMA, P.L. 108-173)	• Moved full-benefit dual eligible beneficiaries from Medicaid to Medicare Part D. • Required maintenance of effort (MOE) payments for dual eligible drug costs—Phased-Down State Contribution (clawback). • Revised the best price definition to exempt discount card drug sales and Medicare Parts C and D drug sales.
Deficit Reduction Act of 2005 (DRA, P.L. 109-171)	• Revised the methodology for determining FULs for multiple source drugs to 250% of the average manufacturer price (AMP). • Authorized the Secretary to provide AMP data and to create a website for disseminating AMP data to states and the public. • Revised the multiple source drug definition by reducing the number of FDA-rated substitutes from three to two. • Permitted states to increase cost-sharing on certain benefits including drugs. • Revised AMP definition to exclude manufacturers' prompt payment discounts to wholesalers. • Required additional state reporting and CMS reports to Congress on state drug prices. • Authorized the Secretary to contract for a national survey of retail drug prices. Survey data was to be available to states on a monthly basis. • Required states to collect and report utilization data for multiple and single source physician administered drugs so that Medicaid rebates could be collected on sales of those drugs.
Medicare Improvements for Patients and Providers Act of 2008 (MIPPA, P.L. 110-275)	• Reinstated the pre-DRA FUL methodology until September 30, 2009. • Temporarily prohibited the Secretary from imposing the DRA FUL methodology until after October 1, 2009. • Temporarily prohibited the Secretary from making AMP data publically available until after October 1, 2009. • Required Medicare Part D plans to cover two drug classes commonly used by dual eligibles that were often covered by Medicaid.

Table 16. (Continued)

Public Law	Summary of Major Outpatient Prescription Drug Provisions
American Recovery and Reinvestment Act of 2009 (ARRA, P.L. 111-5)	• Temporarily increased FMAP, which temporarily reduced clawback for dual eligibles' drug costs.
Patient Protection and Affordable Care Act (ACA, P.L. 111-148, as amended)	• Increased Medicaid rebate percentages with the federal government receiving the increased rebate percentage. • Revised FUL methodology for multiple source drugs to not less than 175% of AMP. • Required manufacturers to pay Medicaid rebates on prescription drugs provided under managed care contracts. • Extended additional rebate requirements to line extension products. • Capped manufacturers' maximum rebate obligation. • Revised definition of AMP to exclude price manufacturer concessions.
Education, Jobs, and Medicaid Assistance Act (EJMAA, P.L. 111-226)	• Clarified the definition of AMP to include sales for 5i drugs,a which generally are not dispensed through retail community pharmacies.

Source: CRS analysis of public laws.

[a] 5i drugs are not delivered to patients as oral solid dose forms but are inhaled, infused, instilled, implanted, or injected. SSA Sec. 1927(k)(l)(B)(i)(IV).

Omnibus Budget Reconciliation Act of 1990 and the Veterans Health Care Act of 1992

Omnibus Budget Reconciliation Act of 1990 (OBRA90, P.L. 101-508) established the Medicaid drug rebate program, which assured Medicaid programs would receive the best price. OBRA90 required drug manufacturers that wanted to sell their drugs to Medicaid enrollees to enter into rebate agreements with the Secretary on behalf of the states.[124] Under the agreements, pharmaceutical manufacturers must provide Medicaid programs with rebates on drugs purchased for Medicaid beneficiaries. Under the terms of the rebate agreements, manufacturers had to give state Medicaid agencies either their best price or a rebate.

After OBRA90 was passed, federal law enabled Medicaid agencies and the federal government to purchase prescription drugs at the lowest market price (best price). An unintended consequence was that certain public health programs, the Department of Veteran's Health Affairs (VHA), the Department of Defense (DOD), and the Public Health Service (PHS) faced sharply higher drug prices. Because Medicaid best price requirements, if pharmaceutical companies gave the DOD, VHA, and PHS providers lower prices, then drug companies would be obligated to sell those products to Medicaid at that same lowest price. Although the percentages of drug manufacturer sales to DOD, PHS programs, and VHA were small, Medicaid accounted for about 12% overall drug sales. Thus, after 1990, when the Medicaid best price provision was implemented, drug manufacturers substantially increased prices to DOD, VHA, and PHS providers.

Congress corrected the oversight by passing the Veterans Health Care Act of 1992 (VHCA, P.L. 102-585). VHCA amended the SSA to exclude certain sales at nominal prices from the Medicaid best price determination and the Medicaid rebate calculation.[125]

Medicare Prescription Drug Improvement and Modernization Act of 2003

Medicare Prescription Drug Improvement and Modernization Act of 2003 (MMA, P.L. 108-173) implemented many prescription drug and other Medicare program changes, but the most far-reaching was the addition of the voluntary outpatient prescription drug benefit for Medicare beneficiaries, Part D. MMA also had an important Medicaid provision that moved outpatient drug coverage for full benefit dual eligibles from Medicaid to Medicare Part D.[126] Although Medicare Part D assumed coverage and payment for dual eligible beneficiaries, MMA contained a maintenance-of-effort provision that required states to continue to pay the majority of dual eligibles' prescription drug costs.[127] In addition, MMA revised the AMP definition to exclude sales to Medicare Part D drug sponsors (Part D plans) in determining AMP.

Deficit Reduction Act of 2005

DRA made a number of changes to Medicaid drug policies. One of these changes was modifying the formula for setting multiple source drug FULs. DRA § 6001 required the Secretary to use a new formula for multiple source drug FULs beginning January 1, 2007. The new FUL formula was to equal

250% of the AMP of the least costly therapeutic equivalent.[128] AMP was defined under DRA to be the average price paid to the manufacturer by wholesalers for drugs distributed to the retail pharmacy class of trade.

Before the new DRA FUL formula could be implemented, two national pharmacy associations filed a complaint challenging the DRA's FUL proposed rule on the ground that the new FULs would generally be below community pharmacies' drug acquisition costs.[129] The court issued a preliminary injunction in December 2007 that prohibited CMS from setting FULs for Medicaid covered generic drugs based on AMP, and from disclosing AMP data except within HHS or to the Department of Justice.[130] The court's 2007 injunction was for an indefinite period and was in place when ACA became law on March 23, 2010, but has since been lifted.[131] CMS lacked authority to use the pre-DRA formula, which expired September 30, 2009, for setting FULs, and CMS also was unable to use the DRA authority because it was prohibited by the Medicare Improvements for Patients and Providers Act of 2010 (MIPPA, P.L. 110-275). Just before the MIPPA-authority for using pre-DRA FULs expired on September 30, 2009, CMS issued FULs. The FULs in place now were set in September 2009.

In addition, DRA made the following changes:

- reduced the required number of multiple source products rated by the FDA as therapeutic and pharmaceutically equivalent from three to two;
- required manufacturers to report AMP to HHS;
- permitted the Secretary to contract for a retail drug price survey that would allow estimation of a nationwide average consumer drug price, net of all discounts and rebates;
- disclosed AMP to states and the public;
- revised the AMP definition; and
- required states to collect and submit data on physician administered drugs.

Medicare Improvements for Patients and Providers Act of 2010

MIPPA § 203 required the Secretary to use the pre-DRA FUL formula for setting federal multiple source drug reimbursement through September 30, 2009. The pre-DRA FUL formula was in effect prior to December 31, 2006. Under this formula, FULs were set at 150% of published prices for the least costly therapeutic equivalent.[132] In addition, the Secretary was prohibited from making AMP prices publicly available prior to September 30, 2009.

American Recovery and Reinvestment Act of 2009

American Recovery and Reinvestment Act of 2009 (ARRA, P.L. 111-5) § 5001 temporarily protected states from FMAP decreases and increased federal matching rates for the recession period.[133] ARRA defined the recession period for the FMAP increase as the period that began with the first quarter of FY2009 (October 1, 2008) and ended with the first quarter of FY2011 (December 31, 2010). During the recession period, states were held harmless from FMAP declines and all states received an across-the-board 6.2 percentage point increase. In addition, certain qualifying states received an additional unemployment-related increase. The Secretary determined that state MOE requirements under MMA for dual eligible drug expenditures were subject to the temporary FMAP increase.[134] The ARRA temporary FMAP increase was extended for an additional by two quarters (until June 30, 2011) by the Education, Jobs and Medicaid Assistance Act (EJMAA, P.L. 111-226).[135]

Patient Protection and Affordable Care Act

Beginning January 1, 2010, with certain exceptions, ACA § 2501 increased the flat rebate percentage used to calculate Medicaid's basic rebate for single source and innovator multiple source outpatient prescription drugs from 15.1% to 23.1% of AMP. The basic rebate percentage for multiple-source, non-innovator, and all other drugs was increased from 11% to 13% of AMP.[136]

ACA also required the Secretary to recover the additional funds states received from drug manufacturers from increases in the basic Medicaid rebates. The Secretary is authorized to reduce Medicaid payments to states for the additional prescription drug rebates that resulted from increases in the minimum rebate percentages—the difference between 15.1% of AMP and 23.1% of AMP for single source products and the difference between 11% and 13% for generic products.[137] ACA requires the Secretary to estimate the additional rebate amounts to recover from states based on utilization and other data. In addition, when it is determined that the recovered amount from a state for a previous quarter under-estimated the actual rebate amount (state share) the Secretary is required to make further adjustments to recover the additional rebates from states. These state payment reductions are considered overpayments to the state and offset against states' regular Medicaid draw, similar to other overpayments. They are not subject to reconsideration.

Moreover, ACA required drug manufacturers to pay rebates to states on drugs dispensed to Medicaid beneficiaries who received care through Medicaid managed care plans, similar to the way rebates are required under previous law for FFS beneficiaries.[138] Medicaid capitation rates paid by states to managed care plans were to be adjusted to include these rebates.[139] Medicaid managed care plans are subject to additional reporting requirements such as submitting data to states on the total number of units of each dose, strength, and package size by National Drug Code (NDC) for each covered outpatient drug.[140] Medicaid managed care plans can use formularies as long as there are exception processes so that excluded drugs are available through a prior authorization process.

With certain exceptions, ACA required that additional rebates for new formulations of single source or innovator multiple source drugs, which are referred to as *line extensions.*[141] Essentially, the additional (inflation) rebates for line extensions products were to be calculated as if the product was the original product. In this way the additional (inflation) rebates is the greater of the basic rebate for new products or the AMP of the new drug multiplied by highest additional (inflation) rebate for any strength of the original product (calculated for each dose and strength of the product).[142] However, ACA limited the total rebate liability for each dosage form and strength of an individual single source or innovator multiple source drug to no more than 100% of that drug's AMP. Other features of the drug rebate program, such as Medicaid's best price requirement, were unchanged by ACA. ACA was amended before it was enacted to clarify that the calculation of the additional rebate for new formulations of existing drugs (line extensions) applied to single source or innovator multiple source drugs only in oral solid dosage forms.[143]

ACA § 2502 required that smoking cessation drugs, barbiturates, and benzodiazepines be removed from Medicaid's excluded drug list. When this provision took effect beginning January 1, 2014, states that covered prescription drugs were required to cover barbiturates, benzodiazepines, and smoking cessation products for most Medicaid beneficiaries.

ACA § 2503 amended Medicaid law to require the Secretary to establish multiple source drug FULs at 175% or more of the weighted average (determined on the basis of utilization) of the most recently reported monthly AMPs.[144] ACA restored the pre-DRA definition of multiple source drugs as at least three therapeutic and pharmaceutically equivalent products.[145] ACA also included technical changes to the FUL formula, such as a smoothing process to reduce short-term volatility, and clarified that AMP excludes the following:

- customary prompt pay discounts to wholesalers;
- bona fide service fees paid by manufacturers to wholesalers and RCPs, such as distribution service fees, inventory management fees, product stocking allowances, and administrative services agreements and patient care programs (medication compliance and patient education programs);
- reimbursement by manufacturers for recalled, damaged, expired, or unsaleable returned goods; and
- payments received from, and rebates or discounts to, large purchasers such as PBMs, managed care plans, health maintenance organizations, insurers, hospitals, clinics, mail-order pharmacies, long-term care providers, manufacturers, or any other entity that does not conduct business as a wholesaler or a RCP.

ACA § 2503 modified the AMP definition further by replacing the retail class of trade terminology with RCPs.[146] This change excluded from drug manufacturers' AMP calculation sales to many non-traditional retail outlets, such as mail order, nursing homes, LTC pharmacies, and PBMs. Excluding drug sales through these outlets from the AMP calculation had the effect of raising AMP, thus increasing Medicaid rebates. Moreover, ACA revised the definition of a multiple source drug from one marketed in a state during the rebate period to a product marketed or sold during the rebate period in the United States.[147] ACA expanded drug pricing disclosure requirements to include monthly weighted average AMPs and retail survey prices. Manufacturers are required to report within 30 days of the end of each month of a rebate period the total number of units sold and used by the manufacturer to calculate the AMP for each covered outpatient drug.

Education, Jobs, and Medicaid Assistance Act

EJMAA § 202 amended ACA to include in AMP sales of 5i drugs that generally are not dispensed through retail community pharmacies. This amendment was a technical change to ACA that was made to ensure that AMPs could be calculated and Medicaid rebates could be collected from manufacturers for the 5i drugs even though these products are not typically sold by RCPs.

Selected Medicaid Prescription Drug Issues

This section discusses the following two Medicaid prescription drug issues: (1) new drug prices and (2) the pending final rule implementing ACA changes.

New Drug Prices

The rising cost of new drugs has been an issue in the past and recently has re-emerged with many groups discussing why drug prices are so high and what can be done to control new drug prices. After a period of relatively few new drugs coming to market, drug manufacturers' pipelines are filling and there could be a surge in new drugs coming to market. Many of the new drugs will be biologic products and some or many of these products will be costly. As a result, concern about rising drugs prices might only be beginning. This section briefly discusses the process for setting new drug prices and then discusses Solvaldi®, a new drug launched in 2014 and how Medicaid drug pricing will affect Solvaldi® and possibly other new drugs.

When drug manufacturers launch new single source drug products, they determine a product's price and generally are not subject to statutory or regulatory limits in setting drug prices. In 2013, FDA approved 27 new molecular entities; in 2012, it approved 39.[148] A number of these newly introduced drugs are expensive, and potentially many more are anticipated.[149] And higher initial prices do not preclude manufacturers from raising prices further after the drugs are launched.

Many organizations, patient groups, Members of Congress, insurers, and individuals are concerned about prescription drug costs. Even going back to the 1990s, when costly antiviral drugs were introduced to treat human immunodeficiency virus/acquired immunodeficiency syndrome (HIV/AIDS), there was considerable concern in Medicaid programs about states' ability to pay for these new drugs.[150] In 2009, GAO published a report that found that drug manufacturers substantially increased prices for certain brand-name drugs from 2000 to 2008.[151] GAO attributed the extraordinary price increases to a number of factors, including lack of good therapeutic alternatives, industry consolidation, and unusual events such as key ingredient supply and manufacturing disruptions.[152] Recently, the topic of excessive new drug costs reemerged accompanying the launch of a new, more effective drug for treating hepatitis C virus (HCV), a liver infection.[153] Pharmaceutical manufacturer, Gilead Sciences, Inc. (Gilead) received FDA approval to market Sofobuvir under the brand-name Solvaldi® in December 2013 for the treatment of chronic HCV infection.[154] Solvaldi's® reported list price is approximately $84,000 for a standard 12-week treatment. Patients can require up to 24 weeks of treatment, and it is usually taken in combination with other drugs, pushing the price above $160,000. In October 2014, the FDA approved a second Gilead drug for treating HCV infections, Ledipasvir/Sofosbuvir, marketed under the brand-name, Harvoni®[155]. Gilead set Harvoni's price at approximately $1,125 per pill, which would result in a cost of about $95,000 for a 12-week treatment course.

Gilead's new HCV drugs, Solvaldi® and Harvoni®, are unquestionably expensive, but other drugs necessary to treat other chronic conditions such as cancer, AIDS, and neurological disorders could over the course of treatment or the patient's life exceed the cost of Solvaldi®.[156]

However, the Solvaldi® product launch may differ from the launch of other drugs for the following reasons: shortage of good therapeutic alternatives, increased awareness of HCV prevalence, improved screening, and, in anticipation of Solvaldi's® launch, a backlog of HCV positive individuals who needed treatment. Because many other new drugs, such as cancer drugs, replace an existing product, new cases are diagnosed gradually and a backlog of cases is unusual. With Solvaldi®, many cases were already diagnosed, so there may have been considerable pent-up treatment demand.[157] This surge for HCV treatment put added financial pressure on all payers but proved particularly heavy for Medicaid and Medicare, which cover many HCV positive individuals and differ from the more gradual financial effect of other expensive drugs that recently have come to market.

In addition, the timing of Solvaldi's® FDA approval and introduction might have contributed to the financial hardship Solvaldi® is creating for Medicaid. Solvaldi® was approved by the FDA in early December 2013. Because Solvaldi® was approved as a breakthrough drug it received fast-track review, which shortened the review time and left less time for payers to become aware of the drug and make contract adjustments or otherwise plan for increased costs.[158] Although December is within the federal fiscal year's first quarter, it is very late in the planning cycle for most health insurance contracts, which follow a calendar year. Medicaid managed care plans, Medicare Part D drug plans, and Medicare Part C plans may have been caught off guard by Solvaldi's® early December launch. Moreover, state budgets that would provide state Medicaid matching funds for drugs purchased for Medicaid FFS beneficiaries were well past the budget planning cycle for the current state fiscal year.[159] Medicaid programs cover Solvaldi®, and as an entitlement the program would need to find fiscal resources whether or not the state had considered the cost when preparing the state's Medicaid budget estimate.

Public health care programs, particularly Medicaid, might be more vulnerable to high prices for new drugs than private payers because cost-sharing generally is nominal and coverage is broad, but all payers experience additional costs. Members of Congress have raised concerns about the effect of these new drug treatments on federal and state budgets and the process drug makers use in setting new drug prices.[160] Medicaid and other private organizations have raised similar concerns about Solvaldi's® cost to both federal and state governments.[161] In addition to concerns about Solvaldi®, private insurers and professional associations have noted the financial impact of high drug prices in general.[162]

Medicaid Rebates for Solvaldi®

Gilead participates in the Medicaid rebate program, so Solvaldi is a covered drug. Similar to established single source drugs, Medicaid agencies that purchase Solvaldi® for covered FFS beneficiaries will receive the basic Medicaid rebate for their drug purchases, which is the greater of the drug's best price minus AMP or 23.1% of the product's AMP. The rebate is split between the federal government and states based on the FMAP rate for part of the rebate, and the remainder goes the federal government.[163] As a new product, Gilead will report Solvaldi's base-period AMP on the basis of sales from the first full calendar quarter after the launch date.[164] Also, Gilead will not owe additional Medicaid (inflation) rebates because Solvadi is new and will not have had price increases greater than inflation until at least after the base-period AMP is established. If, or when, Solvaldi's price increases faster than its base-period AMP adjusted for inflation, then Gilead will owe an additional rebate. The additional rebate also is shared by federal and state governments. When Solvaldi® is provided to Medicaid beneficiaries by managed care plans, Gilead would be obligated to pay the basic rebate for those purchases, and the additional Medicaid rebate would be applicable if or when Gilead raised prices faster the inflation adjusted base-period AMP.

In the short term, Medicaid rebates will help to offset some of the initial cost of treating HCVpositive Medicaid beneficiaries, but Medicaid programs anticipate substantial budget effects. In the longer-term, Medicaid's cost for Solvaldi may decrease through competition from other new therapeutically equivalent products. Other drug makers have new drugs in late-stage development that have shown promise in treating HCV.[165] If some of these other new drugs are approved, Medicaid programs will be able to negotiate with all drug manufacturers that offer HCV products to get better deals on HCV drugs. In FFS Medicaid, when competing products come to market state programs may be able to negotiate SRAs for therapeutically comparable products by offering to list one company's drug on the state PDL essentially guaranteeing that company most sales for HVC drugs. Medicaid managed care plans also may be able to negotiate discounts when competing products come to market, either individually or through PBMs. In addition, in some situations, individual and combined multi-state purchasing pools can further increase states' leverage in negotiating additional manufacturer price concessions. Once competition is available, even though other manufacturers may price their drugs comparably to Solvaldi®, Medicaid programs will be able to use PDLs and other techniques to help reduce their Solvaldi expenditures. Even before competition from other products is available, states may limit access to Solvaldi® by requiring that it be used only in limited situations, such as when a beneficiary is free from drug use or when they have advanced disease.

Hypothetical New Drug Pricing Scenario

Gilead's process for determining the launch price for Solvaldi® is not public information. In setting prices, drug manufacturers may consider the costs their new products would offset. Would a chemotherapy drug extend a patient's life a few months or potentially cure the cancer? Would the drug diminish the likelihood of the need for surgery or, in Solvaldi's case, the need for liver transplants in some cases? If the need for liver transplants were significantly reduced, an expensive, even very expensive, drug might save the health system considerable money. [166] Some drug industry executives attribute high drug prices to how the health care industry pays for services and supplies rather than to drug companies attempting to maximize revenue and profit.[167]

Medicaid's drug pricing policies might also contribute to new drug price escalation, particularly for a drug such as Solvaldi® that potentially will treat many Medicaid beneficiaries. Medicaid's two-tiered rebate, with a basic rebate and an additional inflation rebate, might indirectly encourage manufacturers to set higher launch prices to offset or recover the cost of Medicaid rebates by reducing the Medicaid inflation rebate. For a drug like Solvaldi®, for which there is little therapeutic competition and there may be some or considerable pent up demand, a high launch price that builds in some future period price increases might reduce a manufacturer's additional rebate obligations. At launch, the manufacturer has the market to itself. If it did not raise prices, or raised prices modestly, the manufacturer would avoid most or all of Medicaid's additional inflation rebate. As the backlog of cases decreased and other new drugs came to market, competition would increase and Solvaldi® might have to make price concessions to maintain its market position. At that point, Gilead might begin to raise prices much faster, which would provide negotiation room for making price concessions to states through supplemental rebates without reducing profit margins. If the drug manufacturer had not raised Solvaldi's price much while it did not have competition, when new substitute drugs came to market Gilead would have built up some room in its price for Solvaldi® for inflation adjustments that it could use before triggering the inflation rebate. Whether or not drug makers are concerned about recovering Medicaid's inflation rebate or some of all Medicaid rebates is unclear, but a high launch price when there are few competing products may carry few risks for drug manufacturers.

ACA Implementation: Pending Final Rule

CMS published an extensive Medicaid drug rebate (MDR) program proposed rule in February 2012 that offered regulatory guidance on the implementation of ACA's Medicaid prescription drug changes.[168] A final rule is pending but anticipated in 2015. Overall, the proposed rule offers substantial guidance to manufacturers and Medicaid programs on how CMS planned to interpret ACA's statutory changes. CMS sought industry comment on a number of issues, so it is unclear how closely a final rule will follow the proposed rule's guidance. The rule proposed modifying the Code of Federal Regulations sections to implement the Medicaid drug changes required in ACA sections 2501, 2503, 3301, 1101, and 1206.[169] **Table 17** identifies regulations that CMS proposed to modify or create in implementing the ACA changes.

Table 17. CFR Sections Affected by ACA MDR Proposed Rule

Code of Federal Regulations (CFR) §	Title
§ 447.500	Basis and Purpose
§ 447.502	Definitions
§ 447.504	Determination of Average Manufacturer Price
§ 447.505	Determination of Best Price
§ 447.506	Authorized Generic Drugs
§ 447.507	Identification of 5i Drugs
§ 447.508	Exclusion from Best Price of Certain Sales at a Nominal Price
§ 447.509	Medicaid Drug Rebates
§ 447.510	Requirements for Manufacturers
§ 447.511	Requirements for States
§ 447.512	Drugs: Aggregate Upper Limits of Payment
§ 447.514	Upper Limits for Multiple Source Drugs
§ 447.516	Upper Limits for Drugs Furnished as Part of Services
§ 447.518	State Plan Requirements, Findings, and Assurances
§ 447.520	Conditions Relating to Physician-Administered Drugs
§ 447.522	Optional Coverage of Investigational Drugs and Other Drugs Not Subject to Rebate

Source: CRS Analysis of CMS Proposed Rule, Medicaid Program: Covered Outpatient Drugs, 77 *Federal Register*, 5318, February 2, 2012.

In the proposed rule, CMS requested comments from industry on a number of issues. CMS proposed to clarify its existing guidance on a number of issues, such as the definitions section. Many of the proposed changes were intended to clarify existing rules to enhance consistency among drug manufacturers and Medicaid programs.

Other proposed changes sought to more closely align CMS's policy with existing FDA drug guidance. CMS also proposed substantial changes to AMP and best price that were aimed at assisting manufacturers in computing and reporting these prices consistently. Although the proposed rule changes were extensive, only the following three new sections added to the CFR subpart: Identification of 5i Drugs (42 CFR §§ 447.504(d) and 447.507), Medicaid Drug Rebate (42 CFR § 447.509), and Requirements for States (42 CFR § 447.511).[170]

A potential major change would be the inclusion of territories as states, which would require territory Medicaid programs to comply with all the state MDR program requirements.

CMS estimated that states and the federal government would save $17.7 billion over five years from implementation of the proposed changes ($13.7 billion to the federal government and $4 billion to the states).[171]

CMS also estimated that drug manufacturers, states, and managed care plans would incur about $81.4 million in costs over the period FY2010-FY2012 in implementing the changes.[172]

CONCLUSION

In general, FFS rebates have been effective in helping to control Medicaid FFS drug expenditures. Overall, FFS outpatient drug expenditures have decreased and Medicaid is able to buy drugs for lower prices than Medicare Part D plans and most other federal programs. Congress has been instrumental in establishing Medicaid drug authority to ensure Medicaid pays some of the lowest prescription drug prices. Congress authorized creation of the infrastructure to manage, monitor, and enforce prescription drug pricing. Congress also extended authority for Medicaid to receive rebates on drugs provided to beneficiaries in managed care, and this has resulted in the rapid movement of prescription drug coverage from FFS Medicaid to Medicaid managed care. The percentage of FFS prescription drug claims has fallen from approximately 10% in 2010 to less than 50% in 2013.

The movement of prescription drug coverage from FFS to managed care plans could make oversight of the Medicaid prescription drug benefit more difficult. States will be able to collect rebates under managed care contracts, although it is unclear how state supplemental rebates will align with managed care plan (or, more likely, PBM) negotiations with drug wholesalers and manufacturers.

Under managed care contracts, states generally delegate some or all DUR and program integrity oversight to managed care plans. Will states be able to conduct DUR and appropriate monitoring comparable to FFS drug benefits? If states and the federal government already procure drugs at some of the best prices, will it be possible for managed care plans and their subcontractor PBMs to reduce costs further? Or will savings come from creating obstacles to beneficiaries receiving covered drugs through utilization controls?

Appendix A. FY2012 State FFS Drug Claims

Table A-1. FY2012 Medicaid FFS Drug Claims (by drug category and state)

State	Claims (x000)			
	Single Source	Non-innovator Multiple Source (Generic)	Innovator Multiple Source	Total
Alaska	156	674	90	919
Alabama	1,189	6,460	634	8,283
Arkansas	726	3,603	432	4,761
Arizona	NA	NA	NA	NA
California	601	3,121	309	4,031
Colorado	3,184	13,373	2,246	18,803
Connecticut	2,020	5,782	708	8,509
District of Columbia	313	713	78	1,104
Delaware	401	1,729	167	2,296
Florida	2,380	11,129	2,576	16,086
Georgia	910	5,967	357	7,235
Hawaii	2	0	21	24
Iowa	666	3,532	483	4,681
Idaho	278	1,430	154	1,862
Illinois	3,082	17,127	1,467	21,676
Indiana	1,849	9,299	953	12,100
Kansas	339	1,453	167	1,959
Kentucky	253	1,655	137	2,045
Louisiana	2,375	7,983	1,114	11,473
Massachusetts	899	6,443	508	7,850
Maryland	583	2,518	276	3,377
Maine	1,055	4,423	458	5,937
Michigan	989	5,052	862	6,903
Minnesota	436	2,435	261	3,132
Missouri	2,143	9,937	1,159	13,238
Mississippi	799	4,056	503	5,357
Montana	141	686	78	905
North Carolina	2,683	11,360	1,396	15,439
North Dakota	52	495	75	622
Nebraska	361	2,444	235	3,040
New Hampshire	193	869	108	1,170
New Jersey	606	2,070	232	2,908
New Mexico	44	315	32	391
Nevada	215	1,044	94	1,353

Table A-1. (Continued)

State	Claims (x000)			
	Single Source	Non-innovator Multiple Source (Generic)	Innovator Multiple Source	Total
New York	3,876	20,127	2,118	26,121
Ohio	921	5,182	641	6,743
Oklahoma	865	5,209	498	6,572
Oregon	254	1,648	174	2,076
Pennsylvania	923	6,110	644	7,677
Rhode Island	57	424	32	514
South Carolina	464	2,183	322	2,970
South Dakota	91	369	43	502
Tennessee	2,029	10,252	1,001	13,282
Texas	4,838	17,208	3,152	25,198
Utah	371	2,015	191	2,577
Virginia	481	3,200	311	3,992
Vermont	259	1,008	142	1,408
Washington	744	4,544	438	5,726
Wisconsin	1,823	9,720	1,134	12,677
West Virginia	1,065	3,946	427	5,438
Wyoming	92	411	46	548
National Total	51,076	242,732	29,684	323,492

Source: CRS analysis of CMS Medicaid FFS prescription DUR reports submitted by each state.

Notes: NA=not applicable. States are required to submit annual Medicaid DUR survey reports, § 1927(g)(3)(D). Arizona has a statewide SSA § 1115 Medicaid managed care waiver. Under the waiver, most services are provided under capitation agreements. Arizona did not report FFS drug utilization data in FY2012. In addition, Hawaii has a statewide § 1115 Medicaid managed care waiver where most beneficiaries are enrolled in managed care. Hawaii also reports minimal FFS drug utilization data. A number of other states use § 1115 waivers to provide services to some Medicaid beneficiaries. All states have some managed care contracts that include drug benefit coverage. Managed care drug expenditure analysis is beyond the scope of this report.

APPENDIX B. FY2012 FFS DRUG PAYMEMT

Table B-1. FY2012 FFS Drug Payment (by drug category and state)

State	Total Payment:a Single Source (in $ millions)	Total Payment:a Innovator Multiple Source (in $ millions)	Total Payment:[a] Non-innovator (Generic) (in $ millions)	Total Payment:[a] All Drug Categories (in $ millions)	Average Payment:[b] All Drug Categories	Average Payment:[b] Brand Name Drug	Average Payment:[b] Generic Drug
Alaska	$42.02	$13.30	$14.01	$69.32	$75.41	$225	$20.79
Alabama	$307.12	$75.33	$130.05	$512.50	62	$210	$20
Arkansas	$176.00	$58.06	$80.39	$314.44	$66.05	$202	$22.31
Arizona	NA	NA	NA	NA	NA	NA	NA
California	$183.40	$57.60	$83.69	$324.69	$80.54	$265	$26.82
Colorado	$1,441.35	$677.75	$352.20	$2,471.29	$131.43	$390	$26.34
Connecticut	$498.00	$106.61	$130.94	$735.56	$86.44	$222	$22.65
District of Columbia	$79.89	$13.63	$15.47	$108.99	$98.70	$239	$21.70
Delaware	$111.04	$28.51	$30.83	$170.38	$74.21	$246	$17.83
Florida	$870.20	$300.53	$157.80	$1,328.54	$82.59	$236	$14.18
Georgia	$299.03	$33.05	$94.41	$426.48	$58.95	$262	$15.82
Hawaii	$0.80	$0.41	$0.09	$1.30	$53.53	$51	$181.90
Iowa	$161.06	$73.54	$46.88	$281.48	$60.13	$204	$13.27
Idaho	$76.51	$29.01	$28.13	$133.65	$71.77	$244	$19.67
Illinois	$776.82	$136.66	$288.05	$1,201.54	$55.43	$201	$16.82
Indiana	$509.25	$133.61	$125.69	$768.55	$63.51	$230	$13.52
Kansas	$104.11	$28.53	$25.84	$158.47	$80.88	$262	$17.79
Kentucky	$64.29	$20.20	$26.03	$110.52	$54.03	$217	$15.72
Louisiana	$604.23	$161.17	$246.50	$1,011.90	$88.20	$219	$30.88
Massachusetts	$304.97	$71.57	$104.54	$481.08	$61.29	$268	$16.23

Table B-1. (Continued)

State	Total Payment:a Single Source (in $ millions)	Total Payment:a Innovator Multiple Source (in $ millions)	Total Payment:[a] Non-innovator (Generic) (in $ millions)	Total Payment:[a] All Drug Categories (in $ millions)	Average Payment:[b] All Drug Categories	Average Payment:[b] Brand Name Drug	Average Payment:[b] Generic Drug
Maryland	$248.04	$45.97	$76.10	$370.12	$109.59	$342	$30.23
Maine	$150.38	$42.09	$31.45	$223.92	$37.72	$127	$7.11
Michigan	$406.45	$148.42	$81.93	$636.79	$92.25	$300	$16.22
Minnesota	$151.15	$58.85	$54.55	$264.55	$84.46	$301	$22.40
Missouri	$650.50	$183.57	$261.09	$1,095.17	$82.73	$253	$26.27
Mississippi	$226.55	$62.80	$123.75	$413.09	$77.11	$222	$30.51
Montana	$39.79	$13.49	$13.50	$66.78	$73.83	$244	$19.68
North Carolina	$781.94	$216.80	$232.73	$1,231.47	$79.77	$245	$20.49
North Dakota	$1.73	$9.59	$25.06	$36.37	$58.47	$89	$50.59
Nebraska	$96.78	$29.19	$37.49	$163.45	$53.78	$211	$15.34
New Hampshire	$56.63	$22.20	$11.96	$90.79	$77.60	$262	$13.76
New Jersey	$285.06	$25.58	$34.56	$345.20	$118.70	$370	$16.70
New Mexico	$9.90	$3.11	$5.24	$18.25	$46.66	$172	$16.62
Nevada	$7.76	$16.93	$23.46	$48.15	$35.57	$80	$22.46
New York	$1,039.06	$230.76	$126.76	$1,396.58	$53.47	$212	$6.30
Ohio	$289.98	$130.95	$82.19	$503.12	$74.61	$270	$15.86
Oklahoma	$251.66	$65.80	$102.46	$419.92	$63.89	$233	$19.67
Oregon	$82.33	$32.28	$29.75	$144.36	$69.52	$268	$18.05
Pennsylvania	$287.85	$89.03	$77.71	$454.58	$59.22	$241	$12.72
Rhode Island	$10.72	$3.48	$4.93	$19.13	$37.22	$158	$11.63
South Carolina	$123.04	$39.69	$30.55	$193.28	$65.09	$207	$14.00
South Dakota	$19.55	$5.92	$7.75	$33.22	$66.17	$191	$21.03
Tennessee	$472.76	$148.89	$147.59	$769.23	$57.91	$205	$14.40

State	Total Payment:[a] Single Source (in $ millions)	Total Payment:[a] Innovator Multiple Source (in $ millions)	Total Payment:[a] Non-innovator (Generic) (in $ millions)	Total Payment:[a] All Drug Categories (in $ millions)	Average Payment:[b] All Drug Categories	Average Payment:[b] Brand Name Drug	Average Payment:[b] Generic Drug
Texas	$904.88	$387.07	$315.63	$1,607.58	$63.80	$162	$18.34
Utah	$99.77	$25.92	$52.09	$177.78	$69.00	$224	$25.85
Virginia	$116.74	$39.86	$47.77	$204.38	$51.20	$198	$14.93
Vermont	$74.50	$30.36	$26.62	$131.49	$93.36	$262	$26.42
Washington	$220.65	$60.63	$76.25	$357.53	$62.44	$238	$16.78
Wisconsin	$428.52	$183.63	$164.19	$776.34	$61.24	$207	$16.89
West Virginia	$227.15	$49.79	$57.12	$334.07	$61.43	$186	$14.48
Wyoming	$27.93	$7.50	$6.94	$42.36	$77.26	$258	$16.89
National Total	$14,399.83	$4,429.21	$4,350.71	$23,179.75	$71.65	$233	$17.92

Source: CRS analysis of CMS's Medicaid FFS prescription DUR reports submitted by each state.

Notes: NA=not available. States are required to submit annual Medicaid DUR survey reports, SSA § 1927(g)(3)(D). Arizona has a statewide SSA § 1115 Medicaid managed care waiver. Under the waiver, most services are provided under capitation agreements. Arizona did not report FFS drug utilization data in FY2012. In addition, Hawaii has a statewide § 1115 Medicaid managed care waiver where most beneficiaries are enrolled in managed care. Hawaii also reports minimal FFS drug utilization data. A number of other states use § 1115 waivers to provide services to some Medicaid beneficiaries. All states have some managed care contracts that include drug benefit coverage. Managed care drug expenditure analysis is beyond the scope of this report.

[a] Payments are prior to all rebates.

[b] Average is computed by dividing total payments by the number of claims.

Appendix C. Medicaid FFS Prescription Drug Claims

Table C-1. Medicaid FFS Prescription Drug Claims and Percentage Changes (by state for FY2011-FY2012)

	Claims		
State	FY2011	FY2012	% Change FY2011-FY2012
Alaska	1,090,065	919,265	-15.67%
Alabama	8,251,336	8,282,742	0.38%
Arkansas	4,783,405	4,760,916	-0.47%
Arizona	NA	NA	NA
California	28,096,569	4,031,456	-85.65%
Colorado	NA	18,802,740	NA
Connecticut	9,362,149	8,509,344	-9.11%
District of Columbia	NA	1,104,234	NA
Delaware	2,216,597	2,296,128	3.59%
Florida	16,027,116	16,086,073	0.37%
Georgia	5,533,604	7,234,756	30.74%
Hawaii	20,804	24,322	16.91%
Iowa	3,225,857	4,681,012	45.11%
Idaho	1,969,678	1,862,185	-5.46%
Illinois	24,909,884	21,676,130	-12.98%
Indiana	12,426,534	12,100,498	-2.62%
Kansas	1,939,663	1,959,248	1.01%
Kentucky	10,807,402	2,045,396	-81.07%
Louisiana	NA	11,473,239	NA
Massachusetts	7,906,969	7,849,649	-0.72%
Maryland	3,267,547	3,377,174	3.36%
Maine	6,496,954	5,936,631	-8.62%
Michigan	8,116,362	6,902,876	-14.95%
Minnesota	3,639,499	3,132,105	-13.94%
Missouri	13,065,496	13,238,206	1.32%
Mississippi	4,288,845	5,357,306	24.91%
Montana	840,623	904,552	7.60%
North Carolina	15,102,134	15,438,663	2.23%

State	Claims		
	FY2011	FY2012	% Change FY2011-FY2012
North Dakota	614,772	622,072	1.19%
Nebraska	2,980,676	3,039,567	1.98%
New Hampshire	1,392,078	1,170,022	-15.95%
New Jersey	6,782,565	2,908,243	-57.12%
New Mexico	387,845	391,140	0.85%
Nevada	1,494,009	1,353,486	-9.41%
New York	56,899,738	26,121,036	-54.09%
Ohio	25,059,033	6,743,267	-73.09%
Oklahoma	6,114,198	6,572,257	7.49%
Oregon	2,069,522	2,076,409	0.33%
Pennsylvania	8,008,227	7,676,726	-4.14%
Rhode Island	559,579	513,844	-8.17%
South Carolina	3,615,790	2,969,587	-17.87%
South Dakota	492,869	502,086	1.87%
Tennessee	12,340,862	13,282,244	7.63%
Texas	33,487,171	25,197,695	-24.75%
Utah	2,603,791	2,576,519	-1.05%
Virginia	1,424,282	3,991,540	180.25%
Vermont	3,353,865	1,408,348	-58.01%
Washington	7,079,566	5,725,881	-19.12%
Wisconsin	5,480,197	12,677,149	131.33%
West Virginia	12,740,938	5,438,045	-57.32%
Wyoming	561,069	548,308	-2.27%
National Total	388,927,734	323,492,317	1.19%
Adjustment for 4 States w/o Claims in FY2011	—	(31,380,213)	—
Adjusted National Total	388,927,734	292,112,104	-24.89%

Source: CRS analysis of CMS's Medicaid FFS prescription DUR reports submitted by each state.

Notes: NA=not available. In FY2011, Arizona, Colorado, the District of Columbia, and Louisiana did not report claims volumes. As a result, the FY2012 claims for those states were subtracted from the total for FY2012 to calculate the percentage change for the states with data for both years (a 33% decrease in the number of FFS claims between FY2011 and FY2012). States are required to submit annual Medicaid DUR survey reports, SSA § 1927(g)(3)(D). Arizona has a statewide SSA § 1115 Medicaid managed care waiver. Under the waiver most services are provided under capitation agreements. Arizona did not report FFS drug utilization data in FY2012. In addition, Hawaii has a statewide § 1115 Medicaid managed care waiver where most beneficiaries are enrolled in managed care. Hawaii also reports minimal FFS drug utilization data. A number of other states use § 1115 waivers to provide services to some Medicaid beneficiaries. All states have some managed care contracts that include drug benefit coverage. Managed care drug expenditure analysis is beyond the scope of this report.

APPENDIX D. STATE GENERIC PRESCRIBING RATES

Table D-1. Medicaid FFS Generic Prescribing Rate (by state for FY2011-FY2012)

	Generic Prescribing Rate	
State	FY2011	FY2012
Alaska	70.10%	73.30%
Alabama	75.44%	77.99%
Arkansas	73.30%	75.70%
Arizona	NA	NA
California	69.40%	71.10%
Colorado	74.73%	77.41%
Connecticut	66.05%	67.95%
District of Columbia	65.00%	64.56%
Delaware	74.00%	76.50%
Florida	67.35%	69.18%
Georgia	68.70%	82.50%
Hawaii	85.00%	88.00%
Iowa	74.10%	75.50%
Idaho	74.00%	76.80%
Illinois	77.20%	79.00%
Indiana	75.90%	76.90%
Kansas	71.60%	82.68%
Kentucky	75.30%	80.90%
Louisiana	NA	70.00%
Massachusetts	80.10%	82.10%
Maryland	72.90%	75.00%
Maine	72.86%	74.50%
Michigan	70.63%	73.18%
Minnesota	76.00%	78.00%
Missouri	73.66%	75.06%
Mississippi	73.00%	76.00%

State	Generic Prescribing Rate	
	FY2011	FY2012
Montana	73.30%	75.80%
North Carolina	71.77%	73.58%
North Dakota	73.57%	79.60%
Nebraska	79.00%	80.00%
New Hampshire	74.90%	74.30%
New Jersey	67.00%	71.00%
New Mexico	79.30%	80.60%
Nevada	71.18%	77.17%
New York	67.00%	77.00%
Ohio	74.86%	76.85%
Oklahoma	76.87%	79.26%
Oregon	77.00%	79.38%
Pennsylvania	77.00%	80.00%
Rhode Island	80.00%	83.00%
South Carolina	71.00%	73.50%
South Dakota	72.70%	75.00%
Tennessee	76.00%	77.18%
Texas	69.87%	68.30%
Utah	77.00%	78.21%
Virginia	69.40%	80.00%
Vermont	73.99%	71.55%
Washington	79.88%	79.36%
Wisconsin	70.40%	76.67%
West Virginia	77.00%	73.00%
Wyoming	73.86%	74.92%
National Average	73.68%	76.30%

Source: CRS analysis of CMS's Medicaid FFS prescription DUR reports submitted by each state. Percentage of all prescriptions where a non-innovator multiple source drug was dispensed.

Notes: NA=not available. States are required to submit annual Medicaid DUR survey reports, SSA § 1927(g)(3)(D). Arizona has a statewide SSA § 1115 Medicaid managed care waiver. Under the waiver, most services are provided under capitation agreements. Arizona did not report FFS drug utilization data in FY2011 and FY2012. In addition, Hawaii has a statewide § 1115 Medicaid managed care waiver where most beneficiaries are enrolled in managed care. Hawaii also reports minimal FFS drug utilization data. FY2011 Louisiana data were unavailable. A number of other states use § 1115 waivers to provide services to some Medicaid beneficiaries. All states have some managed care contracts that include drug benefit coverage. Managed care drug expenditure analysis is beyond the scope of this report.

APPENDIX E. GLOSSARY: MEDICAID DRUG TERMS

Table E-1. Selected Medicaid Prescription Drug Terms

Term	Definition
Actual Acquisition Cost (AAC)	Final cost of drugs to pharmacy after all discounts, rebates, and price concessions (not defined in statute or regulations).
Average Manufacturer Price (AMP)	AMP for a covered outpatient drug for a rebate period (calendar quarter) is the average price paid to the manufacturer for the drug in the United States by (i) wholesalers for drugs distributed to RCPs; and (ii) RCPs that purchase drugs directly from drug manufacturers (SSA § 1927(k)(1)).
Average Wholesale Price (AWP)	Commercially published reference price but not an average price paid by purchasers or charged by wholesalers. AWP is considered a manufacturer's suggested wholesale price to the retailer as listed in published drug industry compendia (not defined in statute or regulations).
Brand Name Drug	Brand name drugs are single source or innovator multiple source drugs (42 CFR § 447.502).
Best Price	Best price for single source and innovator multiple source drugs is the lowest price available from a manufacturer during the rebate period to any U.S. entity in any pricing structure (including capitated payments) for the same quarter as the AMP is reported (42 CFR § 447.505).
Consumer Price Index— Urban (CPI-U)	CPI-U is the index of consumer prices developed and updated by the U.S. Department of Labor. It is the CPI for all urban consumers (U.S. average) for the month before the beginning of the calendar quarter for which the rebate is paid (42 CFR § 407.502).
Estimated Acquisition Cost (EAC)	EAC is a Medicaid agency's best estimate of the price generally and currently paid by providers for a drug marketed or sold by a particular manufacturer or labeler in the package size of drug most frequently purchased by providers (42 CFR § 407.502).
Generic Drug	Non-innovator multisource drugs. The term generic drug is not defined in statute (OIG).
Innovator Multiple Source Drug	An innovator multiple source drug is a drug that was originally marketed under an original NDA approved by the FDA, including an authorized generic drug. It includes a drug product marketed by any cross-licensed producers, labelers, or distributors operating under the NDA and a covered outpatient drug approved under a product license approval (PLA), establishment license approval (ELA), or antibiotic drug approval (ADA) (42 CFR § 407.502).

Term	Definition
Multiple Source Brand Name Drugs	Multiple source brand name drugs are innovator multiple source drugs; brand name drugs that have generic equivalents (OIG).
National Drug Acquisition Cost (NADAC)	NADAC is the national price benchmark of the costs that pharmacies pay to acquire prescription and OTC drugs. It is based on invoice cost data collected from pharmacies that reflect actual drug purchases (CMS, Draft Methodology for Calculating the National Average Drug Acquisition Cost, Part II, May 2012).
National Drug Codes (NDCs)	NDCs are unique 11-digit codes that identify each drug manufacturer, drug strength, and package size. Medicaid uses NDCs identify unique formulations of each drug, including the manufacturer, strength, and package size (OIG).
Non-innovator Multiple Source Drug	Non-innovator multiple source drugs are also known as generic drugs and are defined as (1) a multiple source drug that is not an innovator multiple source drug or a single source drug, (2) a multiple source drug that is marketed under an abbreviated NDA or an abbreviated antibiotic drug application, or (3) a drug that entered the market before 1962 that was not initially marketed under an original NDA (42 CFR § 407.502).
Retail Community Pharmacy (RCP)	Retail community pharmacies are state-licensed independent pharmacies, chain pharmacies, supermarket pharmacies, or mass merchandiser pharmacies that dispense medications to the general public at retail prices. RCPs do not include pharmacies that dispense prescription medications to patients primarily through the mail-order, nursing home pharmacies, long-term care facility pharmacies, hospital pharmacies, clinics, charitable or not-for-profit pharmacies, government pharmacies, or PBMs (SSA § 1927(k)(10).
Single Source Drug	A single source drug is a covered outpatient drug produced or distributed under an original NDA approved by the FDA, including a drug product marketed by any cross-licensed producers or distributors operating under the NDA. It also includes a covered outpatient drug approved under a biological license application, PLA, ELA, or ADA (42 CFR § 407.502).
Wholesale Acquisition Cost (WAC)	A drug or biological's wholesale acquisition cost is the manufacturer's list price for the drug or biological to wholesalers or direct purchasers in the United States, not including prompt pay or other discounts, rebates or reductions in price, for the most recent month for which the information is available, as reported in wholesale price guides or other publications of drug or biological pricing data (SSA § 1847A(c)(6)).

Table E-1. (Continued)

Term	Definition
Wholesaler	A drug wholesaler is engaged in wholesale distribution of prescription drugs to retail community pharmacies, including manufacturers, re-packagers, distributors, own-label distributors, private-label distributors, jobbers, brokers, warehouses (including manufacturer's and distributor's warehouses, chain drug warehouses, and wholesale drug warehouses) independent wholesale drug traders, and retail community pharmacies that conduct wholesale distributions (SSA § 1927(k)(11).

Source: CRS summary of SSA, Code of Federal Regulations, and OIG reports.

End Notes

[1] Department of Health and Human Services Office of Inspector General (OIG), States' Collection of Rebates for Drugs Paid Through Medicaid Managed Care Organizations (OEI-03-11-00480). The Social Security Act § 1903(m)(1)(A) defines a Medicaid managed care organization as a health maintenance organization that contracts with a state Medicaid agency to provide or arrange for health services to eligible individuals.

[2] Best price is the lowest price available from a manufacturer during the rebate period to any U.S. entity in any pricing structure (including capitated payments) for the reporting period. Drug manufacturers are required to report best price and other pricing data to the Centers for Medicare & Medicaid Services (CMS) on a quarterly basis (42 CFR § 447.505).

[3] Supplemental rebates are not required by federal Medicaid law. Supplemental rebates are also referred to as state sidebar rebates. Supplemental rebates are essentially side deals between states and drug makers, but states must share the rebates with the federal government.

[4] Under Medicaid managed care, states prospectively pay a health plan a fixed (capitated) monthly fee for all covered health care services a beneficiary will need, except for services both parties agree are excluded or *carved out*. When certain services are covered by managed care contracts, such as prescription drugs, they are considered *carved in* to the contracts. Medicaid managed care plans reimburse retail pharmacies for drugs dispensed to the Medicaid beneficiaries they cover. The health plan negotiates the amount it will reimburse with pharmacies.

[5] The maintenance of effort provision is called the phased-down state contribution (PSC), SSA § 1935(c)(1).

[6] The five states are California, Kentucky, New York, Ohio, and Texas.

[7] The Food and Drug Administration (FDA) approved a second HCV drug in October 2014, Harvoni®, with comparable pricing to Solvaldi®.

[8] In a recent letter, the National Association of Medicaid Directors (NAMD) asked congressional leaders to address drug prices http://medicaiddirectors.org/sites/medicaiddirectors.org /files/public/namd_sovaldi_letter_to_congress 28-14.pdf.

[9] PBMs help public and private purchasers manage prescription drug benefits. PBMs often negotiate drug prices with pharmacies and drug manufacturers on behalf of health plans

and, in addition to other administrative, clinical, and cost containment services, process drug claims for health plans.

[10] Congressional Budget Office (CBO), *Competition and the Cost of Medicare's Prescription Drug Program*, July 2014.

[11] Ibid.

[12] For more information on Medicaid, see CRS Report R43357, *Medicaid: An Overview,* coordinated by Alison Mitchell.

[13] Centers for Medicare & Medicaid Services (CMS), FY2013 Preliminary Financial Report (CMS Form 64). These expenditure data exclude territory expenditures. For more information on Medicaid expenditures, see CRS Report R42640, *Medicaid Financing and Expenditures*, by Alison Mitchell.

[14] Each state submits a plan that describes how the state addresses Medicaid requirements and options. When states make changes they submit a state plan amendment (SPA) to CMS for approval (SSA § 1902, State Plans for Medicaid Assistance).

[15] Throughout this paper, unless otherwise indicated, references to states include the 50 states and the District of Columbia (DC), but not U.S. territories.

[16] Resources include bank accounts and similar liquid assets as well as real estate, automobiles, and other personal property whose value exceeds specified limits, but usually exclude individuals' primary residences.

[17] The 2013 Federal Poverty Level (FPL) for a family of three was $19,530. For more FPL information, see http://aspe.hhs.gov/poverty

[18] A number of states use Medicaid waivers to extend coverage to other eligibility groups not traditionally eligible. For more information, see http://www.medicaid.gov/Medicaid-CHIP-Program-Information/By-Topics/Waivers/1115/ Section-1115-Demonstrations.html.

[19] For more information on eligibility, see CRS Report R43357, *Medicaid: An Overview*, coordinated by Alison Mitchell.

[20] Henry J. Kaiser Family Foundations, Kaiser Commission on Medicaid and the Uninsured, *The Medicaid Medically Needy Program: Spending and Enrollment Update*, December 2012. States have additional options under the Patient Protection and Affordable Care Act (ACA, P.L. 111-148) to expand Medicaid coverage and exchanges can provide additional health insurance coverage. These options could potentially reach individuals who previously were covered by Medicaid under the medically needy option

[21] A list of Medicaid eligibility groups, including which are mandatory and which are optional, is available at http://www.medicaid.gov/Medicaid-CHIP-Program-Information/By-Topics /Waivers/1115/Downloads/List-ofEligibility-Groups.pdf.

[22] For more information on Medicaid benefits, see CRS Report R43656, *Traditional Benefits and Alternative Benefit Plans Under Medicaid*, by Elicia J. Herz.

[23] In 2012, all states covered outpatient drugs for the categorically needy, and most states covered drugs for both the categorically and medically needy, Kaiser Henry J. Kaiser Family Foundation, State Health Facts, Medicaid Benefits: Prescription Drugs.

[24] The Deficit Reduction Act of 2005 (DRA, P.L. 109-171), amended the SSA to create § 1937, State Flexibility in Benefit Packages. Under SSA § 1937, states have the option to provide health care benefits specifically tailored to certain Medicaid population group needs, target residents in certain state areas, or provide services through specific delivery systems. These benefit packages are referred to as benchmark coverage or benchmark-equivalent coverage. A benchmark means the benefits are at least equal to one of the statutorily specified plans, and benchmark-equivalent means the benefits include certain specified services and the overall benefits are at least actuarially equivalent to one of the statutorily specified

benchmark coverage packages. For more information see, http://www.medicaid.gov /MedicaidCHIP-Program-Information/By-Topics/Benefits/Benchmark-Benefits.html.

[25] CBO, *Offsetting Effects of Prescription Drug Use on Medicare's Spending for Medical Services*, November 2012, http://www.cbo.gov/sites/default/files/cbofiles /attachments /43741-MedicalOffsets-11-29-12.pdf.

[26] A formulary is a list of drugs that the state Medicaid agency has identified as preferred products.

[27] Prior authorization is the process in which patients' providers request approval from the Medicaid agency or its contractor to prescribe a specific drug before that drug can be dispensed.

[28] SSA § 1927(d)((4), Requirements for Formularies.

[29] SSA § 1927(d)(2) List of Drugs Subject to Restriction. Medicaid excluded drugs—referred to as the *excluded drug list*—include the following drugs, drug classes, or drug uses: (a) to treat anorexia, weight loss, or weight gain; (b) to promote fertility; (c) for cosmetic purposes or hair growth; (d) for the relief of coughs and colds; (e) prescription vitamins and mineral products (except prenatal vitamins and fluoride preparations); (f) non-prescription drugs, except for pregnant women when recommended by the SSA § 1905(bb)(2)(A) guideline as U.S. Food and Drug Administration (FDA-) approved OTC monograph series to promote smoking cessation treatment; (g) drugs requiring tests or monitoring that can only be provided by the drug manufacturer, and (k) for the treatment of sexual or erectile dysfunction (ED), unless such agents are FDA-approved to treat conditions other than ED.

[30] Federal financial participation (FFP) is the federal share of state Medicaid expenditures. The QI, TMA, and Abstinence Programs Extension and Hurricane Katrina Unemployment Relief Act of 2005 (P.L. 109-91), § 104 prohibited states from receiving matching payments for ED drugs, unless they were prescribed for other FDA-approved uses (SSA § 1903(i)(21)).

[31] SSA § 1927(d)(7), Non-Excludable Drugs, include the following drugs, drug classes, or drug uses: FDA-approved products to promote smoking cessation, including FDA-approved OTC drugs; barbiturates; and benzodiazepines. Barbiturates and benzodiazepines are drugs prescribed as sedatives and tranquilizers.

[32] Many states use primary care case management (PCCM) arrangements in which pediatricians and other primary care providers receive a small per member per month fee to manage patients' care. PCCM providers are not financially responsible for the cost of beneficiaries' care. PCCM and similar managed care arrangements are most often used for select eligibility groups such as children and adults, but less often for aged, disabled, and blind Medicaid beneficiary groups.

[33] SSA § 1927(j), Exemption from Organized Health Settings. Managed care plans are exempt from the FFS rules when they contract with Medicaid and the drugs they are providing are subject to discounts under the Public Health Service Act § 340B.

[34] A letter from the Secretary to state Medicaid directors provided guidance to states on managed care coverage. The letter informed states that if drugs were covered under FFS Medicaid, they also must be available in Medicaid managed care plan formularies. CMS, State Medicaid Director Letter, Coverage of Protease Inhibitors, June 19, 1996, http://downloads.cms.gov/cmsgov/archived-downloads/SMDL/downloads/smd061996.pdf.

[35] See CMCS letter to state Medicaid directors (SMDL#10-019, ACA#9), *Re: Medicaid Prescription Drugs*, September 28, 2010 at http://www.medicaid.gov/Federal-Policy-Guidance/downloads/SMD10019.pdf.

[36] CBO estimated that 90% of Medicaid drug expenditures were paid under FFS arrangements in FY2010; see *Competition and the Cost of Medicare's Prescription Drug Program*, July 2014.

[37] National Pharmaceutical Council, *Pharmaceutical Benefits Under State Medical Assistance Programs 2007* (last year published), National Pharmaceutical Council, at http://www.npcnow.org/publication/pharmaceutical-. Coverage of smoking cessation products is now required. H2 antagonists are gastrointestinal products to reduce excess acid and treat ulcers.

[38] Some Medicaid beneficiaries in managed care might obtain drugs through pharmacies that are part of a managed care plan. In addition, some beneficiaries in long-term care or other institutions might obtain drugs through pharmacies included in those facilities.

[39] SSA § 1927(e)(4), Establishment of Upper Payment Limits.

[40] 42 CFR § 447.502(3), Definitions. Authorized generic drugs are included as innovator multiple source products.

[41] 42 CFR § 447.502(4), Definitions.

[42] Medicaid law does not specifically define generic drugs. In Medicaid, a non-innovator multiple source drug is considered a generic drug. For more information, see the glossary in Appendix E.

[43] 42 CFR § 447.512(b), Drugs: Aggregate Upper Limits of Payment; Other Drugs.

[44] 42 CFR § 447.304, Adherence to Upper Limits; FFP; and 42 CFR § 447.512, Drugs: Aggregate Upper Limits of Payment.

[45] GAO, *Medicaid Prescription Drugs: CMS Should Implement Revised Federal Upper Limits and Monitor Their Relationship to Retail Pharmacy Acquisition Costs* (GAO-14-68), December 2013.

[46] SSA § 1927(e)(4), Establishment of Upper Limit Payments.

[47] In January 2012, CMS identified 760 drugs with FUL amounts. Federal Medicaid law specifies that drugs subject to FULs must be available for purchase by retail community pharmacies (RCPs) on a nationwide basis. RCPs include chain pharmacies, supermarket pharmacies, and mass merchandiser pharmacies that dispense medications to the general public at retail prices (for more information, see glossary in Appendix E).

[48] SSA § 1927(e)(5), Use of AMP in Upper Payment Limits.

[49] For more information, see CMS's *Draft ACA AMP-Based FUL Methodology and Data Elements Guide to the Draft FUL Files* at http://www.medicaid.gov/Medicaid Downloads/MethodologyGuide-AMP-BasedFULnew.pdf.

[50] SSA § 1927(b)(3). Manufacturers that enter into Medicaid rebate agreements must report quarterly and monthly drug AMPs to CMS. Monthly AMPs are used to set FULs, whereas quarterly AMPs are primarily used to determine rebates.

[51] For more information, see the ACA draft FUL methodology at http://www.medicaid.gov/Medicaid-. CMS issued a proposed rule with further guidance on what sales are included in AMP; 77 *Federal Register* 5318, February 2, 2012.

[52] CMS has not calculated and published FULs since its authority to use the pre-DRA formula expired in September 2009. As discussed below in the section on Medicaid prescription drug laws of this report, changes in multiple source drug FUL policy were made in a number of laws and some of these changes have not been fully implemented.

[53] CMS announced in November 2013 it would make the ACA FUL policies final in July 2014. See http://medicaid.gov/Federal-Policy-Guidance/Downloads/CIB-11-27-2013-FULs.pdf.

[54] CMS June 2014 guidance is available at http://www.medicaid.gov/Medicaid Benefits/Prescription-Drugs/Federal-Upper-Limits.html.

[55] GAO, Medicaid Prescription Drugs: CMS Should Implement Revised Federal Upper Limits and Monitor Their Relationship to Retail Pharmacy Acquisition Costs (GAO-14-68), December 2013.

[56] 42 CFR § 447.512(c).

[57] Actual acquisition cost (AAC) is the final drug cost to the pharmacy after all discounts, rebates, and price concessions (see Glossary in Appendix).

[58] National drug pricing compendia include *First Data Bank*, *Red Book*, and *MediSpan*, GAO, *Medicaid Prescription Drugs: CMS Should Implement Revised Federal Upper Limits and Monitor Their Relationship to Retail Pharmacy Acquisition Costs* (GAO-14-68), December 2013.

[59] Department of Health and Human Services Office of Inspector General (OIG), *Medicaid Drug Price Comparisons: Average Manufacturer Price to Published Prices* (OEI-05-05-00240), July 2005.

[60] OIG, *Medicaid Drug Pricing in State Maximum Allowable Cost Programs* (OEI-03-11-00640), August 2013.

[61] CMS, *Medicaid Covered Outpatient Prescription Drug Reimbursement Information by State*, Quarter ending June 2014. The states without maximum allowable costs were Arizona, Mississippi, Nevada, Oregon, Rhode Island, and Wyoming.

[62] More discussion about the DRA changes and legal and other controversy surrounding federal Medicaid policy on the issue appears in the prescription drug law section of this report.

[63] American Medicaid Pharmacy Administrators Association and the National Association of State Medicaid Directors, *Executive Summary and White Paper on Post AWP [Average Wholesale Price]Pharmacy Pricing and Reimbursement*, November 2009. A court determined that AWPs were not valid pricing benchmarks and as a result the most widely used compendia decided it would cease publishing AWPs by September 2011. Thus, state Medicaid agencies that relied on that compendia would need to switch to another or find a different benchmark.

[64] OIG, *Replacing Average Wholesale Price: Medicaid Drug Payment Policy* (OEI-03-11), July 2011.

[65] SSA § 1927(b)(2)(D)(v).

[66] Ibid.

[67] SSA § 1927(f), Survey of Retail Prices; State Payment and Utilization Rates, and Performance Rankings.

[68] CMS, *Methodology for Calculating the National Average Drug Acquisition Cost (NADAC) for Medicaid Covered Outpatient Drugs*, November 2013.

[69] NADAC files are available at http://www.medicaid.gov/Medicaid Prescription-Drugs/Pharmacy-Pricing.html.

[70] For more information on the CMS average retail consumer price and the average drug acquisition cost survey, see CMS's website, http://www.medicaid.gov/Medicaid-

[71] National Association of Medicaid Directors (NAMD), *Update on Actual Acquisition Cost (ACC)-based Prescription Drug Reimbursement Methodology*, June 2014 at http://medicaiddirectors.org/.

[72] The seven states using an ACC-based rate for ingredient reimbursement were Alabama, Colorado, Delaware, Idaho, Iowa, Louisiana, and Oregon. Delaware was using CMS's NADAC data in setting its Medicaid drug reimbursement rate for ingredient cost.

[73] CMS publishes a summary of state reimbursement formulas at the end of each quarter, *Medicaid Covered Outpatient Prescription Drug Reimbursement Information by State: Quarter ending June 31, 2014* at http://www.medicaid.gov/ Medicaid-CHIP-Program-

Information/By-Topics/Benefits/Prescription-Drugs/State-Prescription-Drug-Resources.html.

[74] All payers pay pharmacists a dispensing fee when they fill a prescription.

[75] 42 CFR § 447.502, Definitions. Dispensing fees are included in state Medicaid plans and are subject to CMS approval.

[76] See CMS, *Medicaid Covered Outpatient Prescription Drug Reimbursement Information by State: Quarter ending June 30, 2014* at http://www.medicaid.gov/Medicaid-CHIP-Program-Information/By-Topics/Benefits/PrescriptionDrugs/State-Prescription-Drug-Resources.html.

[77] The Omnibus Budget Reconciliation Act of 1990 (OBRA90, P.L. 101-508) § 4401, Reimbursement for Prescribed Drugs, established the Medicaid Drug Rebate (MDR) program (see report section, Selected Medicaid Prescription Drug Laws).

[78] See for a sample MDR agreement at http://www.medicaid.gov/MedicaidBenefits/Prescription-Drugs/Downloads/SampleRebate Agreement.pdf.

[79] *Best price* for a single source or innovator multiple source drug is the manufacturer's lowest price available during the rebate period to any entity in the United States in any pricing structure (including capitated payments) in the same quarter for which the AMP is computed. Best price is required to be calculated to include all sales and associated rebates, discounts, and other price concessions unless the sale, discount, or other price concession is specifically excluded (42 CFR § 447.505).

[80] The drugs, drug classes, or drug uses that states have the option to exclude from coverage can be found at SSA § 1927(d)(2).

[81] SSA § 1927(k)(3), Limiting Definition. The general rule is that rebates apply to drugs when they are billed separately, but not when they are reimbursed as part of a claim for another service.

[82] ACA § 2501(c), Extension of Prescription Drug Discounts to Enrollees of Medicaid Managed Care Organizations, and SSA § 1903(m)(2)(C).

[83] SSA § 1927(k)(4). Nonprescription Drugs.

[84] Email response to CRS from the CMS's Center for Medicaid and CHIP, Disabled & Elderly Health Programs Group, Division of Pharmacy, May 2, 2014.

[85] Federal medical assistance percentages (FMAPs) are used to determine the amount of federal matching funds states receive for medical assistance. SSA § 1905(b) identifies the formula the Secretary must use to calculate FMAPs. By statute, FMAPs may vary from 50% to 83%. In FY2015, 7 states had FMAPs of at least 70% and 13 states had 50% FMAPs (http://aspe.hhs.gov/health. For more information, see CRS Report R42941, *Medicaid's Federal Medical Assistance Percentage (FMAP), FY2014*, by Alison Mitchell and Evelyne P. Baumrucker.

[86] For more information on FDA-approved new drug applications, see CRS Report R41983, *How FDA Approves Drugs and Regulates Their Safety and Effectiveness*, by Susan Thaul.

[87] States and the federal government share the basic rebate, according to the FMAP rate for each state, up to 15.1% of AMP. The federal government receives the entire rebate amount between 15.1% and 23.1% of AMP (SSA § 1927(b)(1)(C).

[88] The inflation rate is measured by the consumer price index for all urban consumers (CPI-U). To determine if prices rose faster than inflation, prices in effect on October 1, 1990, are used as a base and compared to prices in effect on the month before the start of the period for which the rebate is to be issued. For drugs that entered the market after October 1, 1990, the base period price is determined by the AMP reported by the manufacturer for the quarter after the drug was launched.

[89] A sample unit rebate amount (URA) calculation for single source and innovator multiple source drugs is available at http://www.medicaid.gov/Medicaid URA-FOR-S-OR-I.pdf.

[90] SSA § 1927(c)(2)(D), Maximum Rebate Amount.

[91] Table 7 displays the total (federal and state) supplemental rebates for FY1997–FY2013.

[92] Drug manufacturers are not required under Medicaid law to pay supplemental rebates, also known as state sidebar rebates.

[93] A Medicaid state plan is an agreement between a state and the federal government describing how a state administers its Medicaid program. The state plan assures that states will abide by federal rules and may claim federal matching funds for its program activities, http://www.medicaid.gov/state-resource-center/medicaid-state-plan-amendments/medicaid-state-plan-amendments.html.

[94] PBMs are entities that contract with health insurers to manage prescription drug benefits. PBMs perform the following activities: claim payment, administrative services, retail pharmacy network development, mail order pharmacy operation, formulary development, manufacturer rebate negotiation, drug interaction monitoring, and discount negotiation.

[95] ACA § 2501(c), Extension of Prescription Drug Discounts to Enrollees of Medicaid Managed Care Organizations.

[96] There is considerable variation in the number of Medicaid beneficiaries covered in states by full-risk managed care contracts, thus states with greater full-risk managed care enrollment and larger managed care rebates may have been more likely to have shown wider fluctuations in reported FFS rebates.

[97] FY2013 Medicaid Statement of Expenditures for the Medical Assistance Program (CMS Form 64 report). Federal law requires supplemental rebates to be shared by states and the federal government in the same proportion as state FMAP rates, which is the same way federally required rebates are shared. The following nine states did not report SRA rebate amounts in FY2013: Alaska, Arizona, Hawaii, Massachusetts, Montana, New Jersey, New Mexico, North Dakota, and South Dakota.

[98] CRS analysis of Medicaid Financial Management Reports (CMS- Form 64 data).

[99] *New York Times*, Generic Drug Makers See a Drought Ahead, December 3, 2012, http://www.nytimes.com/2012/12/ 04/business/generic-drug-makers-facing-squeeze-on-revenue.html?pagewanted=all&_r=0; and *Nature*, The Patent Cliff Steepens, January 2011, http://www.nature.com/nrd/journal/v10/n1/full/nrd3356.html.

[100] Federal Medicaid law was amended by the Medicare Prescription Drug Improvement and Modernization Act of 2003 (MMA, P.L. 109-273), the DRA (P.L. 109-171), and ACA. More modest changes were made by the Medicare Improvements for Patients and Providers Act of 2008 (MIPPA, P.L. 110-275) and American Recovery and Reinvestment Act of 2009 (ARRA, P.L. 111-5). For more information on federal laws affecting Medicaid drug benefits, see the section Selected Medicaid Prescription Drug Laws of this report.

[101] Medicare and Medicaid generally cover different populations, but an estimated 9.3 million low-income individuals were eligible for both programs in November 2013. Two-thirds of dual eligible beneficiaries were at least age 65, and one-third qualified through a disability. There are two dual eligible types, full and partial benefit. The majority of dual eligibles are full benefit, meaning they are eligible for both Medicare benefits and full Medicaid benefits under their state's Medicaid plan. In November 2013, approximately 72% of duals were full-benefit dual eligibles. Data are from CMS's dual eligible tracking (DET) system, December 15, 2013. Dual eligible data from other sources may vary.

[102] American Recovery and Reinvestment Act of 2009 (ARRA, P.L. 111-5), § 5001, Increased Federal Medical Assistance Percentage (FMAP).

[103] PSC is also known as the *clawback* (SSA § 1935(c)(1)). See State Medicaid Director Letter, SMDL 10-004, *Re: Revised Clawback Calculation*, March 5, 2010, http://downloads.cms.gov/cmsgov/archived-downloads/SMDL/ downloads/SMD10004.pdf.

[104] Dual eligible drug costs were shifted from Medicaid to Medicare Part D beginning January 1, 2006.

[105] If per person managed care drug spending (which is not shown separately in Medicaid Statistical Information System data) differs significantly from FFS per person drug spending, then these estimates could be somewhat distorted. Because Medicaid health maintenance organizations (HMOs) enroll many more children and adults than aged or disabled individuals, the exclusion of managed care drug payments might have a greater relative impact on estimates of average spending among children and adults.

[106] CMS FY2012 Medicaid FFS prescription drug utilization review (DUR) reports, http://www.medicaid.gov/Medicaid-CHIP-Program-Information/By-Topics/Benefits /Prescription-Drugs/Drug-Utilization-Review.html.

[107] The average reimbursement was estimated before deducting for national and state-negotiated rebates. A number of other factors can effect average prescription reimbursement, including state Medicaid drug payment policies, the number and basis of eligibility for beneficiaries enrolled in managed care, and other state drug policies such as utilization controls.

[108] The percentage decrease in claims volume is actually about 30%. Four states did not submit data in FY2011, but did in FY2012. When the data for these states is excluded from FY2012 data, the percentage decrease in claims is about 30%.

[109] CBO, *Competition and the Cost of Medicare's Prescription Drug Program*, July 2014.

[110] Arizona has a statewide SSA § 1115 Medicaid managed care waiver. Under the waiver, most services are provided under managed care capitation agreements.

[111] Most states have drug substitution policy (DSP) laws that permit pharmacists to substitute a generically or therapeutically equivalent drug independently without contacting the prescribing physician, unless the physician has specified on the prescription not to make substitutions. Physicians can override DSP by writing on the prescription (or otherwise indicating on electronic prescription), "dispense as written (DAW)," "do not substitute," "medically necessary," "brand only," or something similar. DAW language requirements vary by state http://www.cellcept.com/ WebResources/pdfs/DAW_ALL_STATES.pdf.

[112] States are required to use a committee appointed by the governor to develop the state's Medicaid formulary. The committee must include physicians, pharmacists, and other health professionals. These committees are commonly referred to as *pharmacy and therapeutics committees* (P&T committees), SSA § 1927(d)(4)(A).

[113] CBO, *Competition and the Cost of Medicare's Prescription Drug Program*, July 2014.

[114] SSA § 1927(g)(C), states received 75% FMAP rates during calendar years 1991-1993 for expenditures attributable to adoption of a conforming DUR program.

[115] SSA § 1927(g)(1). General DUR program requirements included assuring that prescriptions were (i) appropriate, (ii) medically necessary, and (iii) not likely to result in adverse medical results.

[116] Medicaid information technology, or *systems mechanization* and *mechanized claims processing and information retrieval systems*, are MMISs, SSA § 1903(a)(3) and regulations at 42 CFR § 433.111.

[117] CMS's FY2012 Comparison and Summary Report, *Medicaid Drug Utilization Review Annual Report,* is available at http://www.medicaid.gov/Medicaid-CHIP-Program-Information/By-Topics/Benefits/Prescription-Drugs/Downloads/2012DUR-Comparison-summary-report.pdf.

[118] Medicaid fiscal agents are private entities that operate and maintain MMIS systems and process FFS claims. Fiscal agents also often provide additional management and administrative support to Medicaid agencies. A summary of state fiscal agent contracts is available at http://medicaid.gov/Medicaid-CHIP-Program-Information/By-Topics/Data-and-Systems/Downloads/MMISFACSR.pdf.

[119] DRA §§ 6041-6043 changed Medicaid cost-sharing rules. Prior to DRA, copayments were prohibited for a number of Medicaid services, beneficiary types, or sites of care. When copayments were permitted they are limited to nominal amounts. For more information on beneficiary groups and services excluded from cost-sharing, see 42 CFR § 447.56, Limitations on Premiums and Cost Sharing.

[120] Nominal amounts are defined in 42 CFR § 447.52-.54. DRA required that beginning in FY2006 nominal amounts were indexed to inflation (as estimated using the medical care component of the consumer price index).

[121] The new options were effective March 31, 2006.

[122] For more information on the Federal Employees Health Benefits Program (FEHBP) health coverage, see CRS Report RS21974, *Federal Employees Health Benefits Program (FEHBP): Available Health Insurance Options*, by Annie L. Mach and Ada S. Cornell.

[123] GAO/HEHS-97-47; *Pharmacy Benefit Managers: FEHBP Plans Satisfied With Savings and Services, but Retail Pharmacies Have Concerns*, February 1997.

[124] For a sample Medicaid Drug Rebate Agreement, see http://www.medicaid.gov/Medicaid-CHIP-ProgramInformation/By-Topics/Benefits/Prescription-Drugs/Downloads/SampleRebateAgreement.pdf.

[125] These agencies include the Department of Veteran's Health Affairs (VHA), the Department of Defense (DOD), the Public Health Service (PHS) and various PHS-funded health programs, and state (non-Medicaid) pharmaceutical assistance programs (SSA § 1927(c)(1)(C)(i)).

[126] As discussed elsewhere in the report, this provision was the Phased-down State Contribution (SSA § 1935(c)(1)); also referred to as the clawback.

[127] In 2006, states paid 90% of dual eligibles' drug costs. The percentage was gradually phased down to 75% beginning in FY2015.

[128] The pre-DRA formula was 150% of the price published in national compendia for the least costly therapeutically equivalent product that could be purchased by pharmacists in quantities of 100 tablets or capsules, plus a reasonable dispensing fee (exceptions applied for other package sizes). DRA substituted 250% of AMP (as computed without regard to customary prompt pay discounts extended to wholesalers) for 150% of published prices. AMP typically is considerably lower than published prices.

[129] See 72 *Federal Register* 39142, Medicaid Program: Prescription Drugs, July 17, 2007. The national pharmacy associations were the National Association of Chain Drug Stores and the National Association of Community Pharmacists. The suit against the Secretary was filed November 7, 2007, https://www.ncpanet.org/pdf/amp_ncpanacdslawsuitcomplaint.pdf.

[130] U.S. District Court for the District of Columbia, National Association of Chain Drug Stores v. Leavitt, (Case 1:07- cv-02017-RCL, December 19, 2007) http://www.cms.gov/Regulations-and-Guidance/Legislation/DeficitReductionAct/ downloads/AMPPIOrder.pdf.

[131] The injunction was lifted December 15, 2010, see http://www.medicaid.gov/Medicaid-CHIP-Program-Information/By-Topics/Benefits/Prescription-Drugs/Downloads/Ordertovacate PI.pdf.

[132] Published prices are those published in national compendia, which include AWP, wholesale acquisition cost (WAC), and direct prices.

[133] For more information, see CRS Report R40223, *American Recovery and Reinvestment Act of 2009 (ARRA, P.L. 111-5): Title V, Medicaid Provisions*, coordinated by Cliff Binder.

[134] For more information, see guidance from CMS to state Medicaid directors, SMDL # 10-004, Re: Revised Clawback Calculations, March 5, 2010, at http://downloads.cms.gov/cmsgov /archived-downloads/SMDL/downloads/ SMD10004.pdf.

[135] CMS issued a Center for Medicaid, CHIP, and Survey and Certification (CMCS) Information Bulletin to state Medicaid directors, FMAP Extension Guidance, August 10, 2010 at https://www.cms.gov/apps/docs/08-18-10-cmcsinformational-bulletin-FMAP-Extension-Guidance.pdf.

[136] States will receive a rebate of 17.1% for certain outpatient single source and innovator multiple source clotting factor drugs and outpatient drugs approved by the FDA exclusively for pediatric indications (SSA § 1927(c)(1)(B).

[137] SSA § 1927(b)(1), Recapture of Total Savings Due to Increase.

[138] For more information on Medicaid managed care plan rebate collections, see OIG, *States' Collection of Rebates for Drugs Paid Through Medicaid Managed Care Organizations* (OEI-03-11-00480), September 2012.

[139] Where applicable (when drugs were included in capitated managed care contracts), states might need to adjust (increase or decrease) their payments to managed care plans to account for drug coverage and rebates.

[140] Drug products are identified and reported using a unique, three-segment number, called the National Drug Code (NDC), which serves as a universal product identifier for drugs. FDA publishes NDCs in the NDC Directory which is updated daily. National Drug Codes are 11-digit numbers that uniquely identifies each drug including the manufacturer (also called the labeler), the product's strength, and package size.

[141] For more information on line extensions and their effect on Medicaid rebates see, OIG, *Review of Additional Rebates for Brand-Name Drugs With Multiple Versions* (A-06-09-00033), March 2010.

[142] New orphan drug formulations are exempted from the additional rebate requirements, regardless of whether the market exclusivity period has expired. Orphan drugs, as designated by § 526 of the Federal Food, Drug, and Cosmetic Act, are used to treat individuals suffering from rare diseases.

[143] For more information on line extensions and their effect on Medicaid rebates, see OIG, *Review of Additional Rebates for Brand-Name Drugs with Multiple Versions* (A-06-09-00033), March 2010.

[144] FULs are set for pharmaceutically and therapeutically equivalent multiple source drugs available nationally through RCPs.

[145] SSA § 1927(e)(4), Establishment of Upper Limits.

[146] SSA § 1927(k)(10), Retail Community Pharmacy.

[147] SSA § 1927(k)(7)(A)(i)(III)).

[148] See FDA, *Novel New Drugs Summary*, January 2014, http://www.fda.gov/downloads/Drugs/ DevelopmentApprovalProcess/DrugInnovation/UCM381803.pdf.

[149] In 2012, more than 500 potential cancer drugs were under investigation, according to a survey by IMS Health, a health care research group—more than five times as many as were being developed in the next biggest category, diabetes. Cancer drugs can have very high prices, with total treatment costs for a course of treatment exceeding $100,000.

[150] In a 1996 letter to state Medicaid directors, CMS provided guidance on coverage of the HIV-AIDS drug class of protease inhibitors, available at http://downloads.cms.gov/cmsgov /archived-downloads/SMDL/downloads/ smd061996.pdf.

[151] GAO, *Brand-name Prescription Drug Pricing: Lack of Therapeutically Equivalent Drugs and Limited Competition May Contribute to Extraordinary Price Increases* (GAO-10-201), December 2009.

[152] The majority of all extraordinary price increases were for drugs priced less than $25 per unit; however, a full course of treatment for some of these drugs could total several thousand dollars.

[153] Hepatitis means inflammation of the liver and also refers to a group of viral infections that affect the liver. The most common types are hepatitis A, hepatitis B, and hepatitis C. Hepatitis C virus (HCV) infection is the most common chronic blood-borne infection in the United States, with an estimated 3.2 million infected individuals.

[154] See FDA approval announcement at http://www.fda.gov/newsevents/newsroom /pressannouncements/ ucm377888.htm. Even though other HCV treatments are available, Solvaldi is considered a breakthrough product, in part because it has fewer side effects, is more effective, and in many cases, does not require accompanying, poorly tolerated interferon drugs.

[155] See FDA approval announcement at http://www.fda.gov/NewsEvents/Newsroom /PressAnnouncements/ ucm418365.htm.

[156] The Centers for Disease Control and Prevention (CDC) estimated the HIV/AIDS lifetime cost to be about $384,000. See *New York Times*, "Is a $1,000 Pill Really Too Much?" August 3, 2014.

[157] Ibid.

[158] Solvaldi was the third drug approved by FDA to receive breakthrough therapy designation (see FDA approval letter). Breakthrough therapies may qualify for a priority review designation, which means FDA's goal is to take action on the marketing application within 6 months of receipt (compared with 10 months under standard review). For more information, see FDA, *Guidance for Industry, Expedited Programs for Serious Conditions – Drugs and Biologics*, May 2014.

[159] State fiscal years generally begin July first. The following four states fiscal years do not follow the July 1-June 30 fiscal year calendar: Alabama and Michigan (Sept. 30), New York (March 31) and Texas (Aug. 30).

[160] Ranking Members of the House Energy and Commerce Committee, requested information from Gilead on Solvaldi's pricing and breakthrough therapy designation, March 20, 2014, at http://democrats.. In addition, the Chairman and Senior Members of Senate Committee on Finance requested information from Gilead on Solvaldi pricing and related issues, July 11, 2014, at http://www.finance.senate.gov/imo/media/doc/Wyden-Grassley%20Document%20 Request%20to%20Gilead%207-11- 141.pdf.

[161] Selected Medicaid-related organizations that have expressed concern about Solvaldi's price include the National Medicaid Director Association (NAMD), and the Medicaid Health Plans of Association (MHPA), and Association of Community Affiliated Plans (ACAP).

[162] These groups include the Pharmaceutical Care Management Association (PCMA) which represents PBMs and the American Association of Health Insurance Plans (AHIP).

[163] SSA § 1927(c)(2) Additional Rebate for Single Source and Innovator Multiple Source Drugs.

[164] SSA § 1927(c)(2)(B) Treatment of Subsequently Approved Drugs.

[165] Barron's Online, *AbbVie: Big Opportunity in Hepatitis C Drugs*, June 17, 2014, at http://online.barrons.com/news/articles/SB5000142405311190392760457963024 2037760268.

[166] Insurers sometimes note that because there is high insurance turnover, there is no guarantee that they will see any future savings from preventing some future catastrophic health event.

[167] Pharmaceutical Research and Manufacturers of America, John Castellani, President and CEO, at http://www.phrma.org/media May 2014.

[168] 77 *Federal Register* 5318, February 2, 2012, Medicaid Program; Covered Outpatient Drugs, Proposed Rule.

[169] The ACA changes would be codified at 42 CFR §§ 447.500-522, Payments for Drugs.

[170] 5i drugs are administered to patients differently than drugs typically available through RCPs such as oral, solid dose forms. The five major drug administration routes not typically available through RCPs all begin with the letter "i"; inhaled, injected, infused, instilled, and implanted.

[171] Medicaid Program; Covered Outpatient Drugs, Proposed Rule, 77 *Federal Register* 5318, February 2, 2012.

[172] Ibid.

In: Medicaid Prescription Drugs
Editor: Sandra Olivia Barton

ISBN: 978-1-63482-522-1

Chapter 2

MEDICAID PRESCRIPTION DRUGS: CMS SHOULD IMPLEMENT REVISED FEDERAL UPPER LIMITS AND MONITOR THEIR RELATIONSHIP TO RETAIL PHARMACY ACQUISITION COSTS*

United States Government Accountability Office

WHY GAO DID THIS STUDY

States reimburse pharmacies for covered outpatient prescription drugs dispensed to Medicaid beneficiaries. For certain multiple-source outpatient prescription drugs, federal matching funds that states receive to reimburse pharmacies are limited by FULs. In 2010, PPACA modified the FUL formula to better reflect pharmacy acquisition costs and thus more effectively control Medicaid expenditures. However, CMS has not yet implemented the PPACA formula and continues to use FULs that were published in September 2009. CMS currently publishes draft PPACA-based FULs. CMS also created the NADACs for states to consider when setting reimbursement rates.

* This is an edited, reformatted and augmented version of the United States Government Accountability Office publication, GAO-14-68, dated December, 2013.

You asked GAO to look at the NADAC and the PPACA-based FULs. This report (1) describes how CMS develops the NADACs and (2) examines how PPACA-based FULs compare to the NADACs. GAO compared draft FULs and NADACs for first quarter 2013 in aggregate across all multiple-source outpatient prescription drugs subject to the FUL. GAO also reviewed CMS documentation and interviewed CMS officials on how the NADACs are developed and PPACA-based FULs are calculated.

WHAT GAO RECOMMENDS

GAO recommends that the CMS Administrator (1) expeditiously implement the PPACA-based FUL formula and (2) monitor the relationship between the PPACA-based FULs and the NADACs on an ongoing basis. HHS concurred with these recommendations.

WHAT GAO FOUND

To develop a national benchmark for retail pharmacy acquisition costs of Medicaid covered outpatient prescription drugs—known as the National Average Drug Acquisition Cost (NADAC)—the Centers for Medicare & Medicaid Services (CMS) within the Department of Health and Human Services (HHS) surveys each month randomly selected retail community pharmacies for invoice data on their actual drug acquisition costs. CMS then calculates an average acquisition cost for each drug based on invoice data received from about 500 to 600 pharmacies. CMS officials expressed confidence in their current process, but noted that some limitations may exist. For example, CMS officials stated the extent to which NADACs reflect rebates and discounts is limited because most occur off-invoice or are not tied to a specific drug purchase. CMS has developed and published more than 5,000 NADACs, which CMS has estimated apply to more than 90 percent of the drug claims reimbursed by Medicaid.

GAO found that the total draft federal upper limits (FUL) amount based on the new formula under the Patient Protection and Affordable Care Act (PPACA) was about 1.4 percent lower than the total NADAC amount in aggregate for 1,035 outpatient drugs subject to the FUL in first quarter 2013.

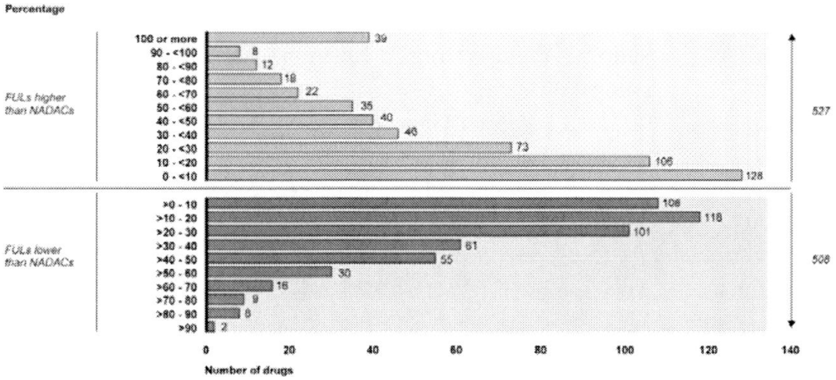

Source: GAO analysis of CMS data.

Comparison of PPACA-Based FULs to NADACs, First Quarter 2013.

GAO found large differences between the total PPACA-based FUL amount and the total NADAC amount for generic and for branded generic versions—brand-name drugs with other versions that can be substituted for one another—of the drugs subject to the FUL in first quarter 2013. GAO found that the total PPACA-based FUL amount for the generic versions was 19 percent higher than the total NADAC amount, but for the branded generic versions was 26 percent lower. GAO's work indicates that CMS is close to having a formula under which FULs would better reflect pharmacy acquisition costs, but continues to apply FULs that were calculated more than 4 years ago. Additionally, the relationship between PPACA-based FULs and NADACs may be affected by several factors, including rebates and discounts that are not reflected on pharmacy invoices. To determine whether GAO's early results of the relationship between the PPACA-based FULs and the NADACs holds over time will require continued monitoring by CMS.

Abbreviations

AAC	Average Acquisition Cost
AMP	average manufacturer price
CMS	Centers for Medicare & Medicaid Services
DRA	Deficit Reduction Act of 2005
FUL	federal upper limit

HHS	Department of Health and Human Services
NADAC	National Average Drug Acquisition Cost
NDC	national drug code
OIG	Office of Inspector General
PCI	per capita income
PPACA	Patient Protection and Affordable Care Act
WAC	wholesale acquisition cost

* * *

December 19, 2013

The Honorable Max Baucus
Chairman
Committee on Finance
United States Senate

The Honorable Charles E. Grassley
Ranking Member
Committee on the Judiciary
United States Senate

Medicaid, a joint federal-state program that finances health care coverage for certain low-income individuals, spent an estimated $40.3 billion on outpatient prescription drugs in fiscal year 2012. State Medicaid programs do not directly purchase prescription drugs but instead reimburse pharmacies for covered prescription drugs dispensed to Medicaid beneficiaries. The federal government provides matching funds to each state for Medicaid expenditures, which cover a portion of the costs of these reimbursements.[1]

For certain multiple-source outpatient prescription drugs with three or more therapeutically and pharmaceutically equivalent versions, the federal government will provide matching funds for reimbursements only up to a maximum amount—known as a federal upper limit (FUL)—in order to control federal Medicaid expenditures on these drugs.[2] While state Medicaid programs may use different methods to reimburse retail pharmacies for covered prescription drugs,[3] for those drugs subject to the FUL the federal government will only provide matching funds to the extent that a state's annual reimbursements do not exceed the sum of the FULs in aggregate.[4] As of September 2009, the formula used by the Centers for Medicare & Medicaid

Services (CMS)—the agency within the Department of Health and Human Services (HHS) that oversees Medicaid—to calculate FULs was based on using 150 percent of the lowest price published in national drug pricing compendia and CMS continues to apply these FULs.[5]

Questions have been raised about whether FULs calculated using prices published in national compendia can effectively control Medicaid expenditures on drugs subject to the FULs because these prices do not reflect pharmacies' actual costs for acquiring these drugs.[6] For example, a 2005 report by the HHS Office of Inspector General (OIG) found that prices in the national compendia exceeded prices based on actual sales by as high as 70 percent.[7] In 2006, Congress required CMS to modify the formula used to calculate FULs. This modified formula was based on using 250 percent of a drug's average manufacturer price (AMP), which represents the average of prices paid to manufacturers and is typically less than prices published in national compendia.[8] However, although CMS published a final rule to implement this formula, implementation did not occur due to a lawsuit filed by pharmacy associations concerned that the modified formula would result in reimbursement below their acquisition costs. These concerns were based in part on work by GAO and the HHS OIG, which generally found that FULs calculated using the modified formula were significantly lower than the average retail pharmacy's acquisition costs.[9] Reimbursing pharmacies below their acquisition costs could in turn affect pharmacies' ability to dispense outpatient prescription drugs to Medicaid beneficiaries and potentially reduce beneficiary access to drugs. In 2010, the Patient Protection and Affordable Care Act (PPACA) again modified the formula for calculating FULs to use no less than 175 percent of a drug's AMP and imposed an effective date of October 1, 2010.[10] CMS has not implemented the PPACA FUL formula yet, but calculates FULs using the formula and publishes these FULs in draft form.[11]

CMS also recently took steps to improve states' access to actual pharmacy acquisition cost data. In June 2010, a working group within the National Association of State Medicaid Directors recommended that CMS develop a single national price benchmark for pharmacy reimbursement based on the average of actual drug acquisition costs to assist states in setting their own reimbursement rates for outpatient prescription drugs. In response to this recommendation, CMS began surveying retail community pharmacies to collect actual prescription drug acquisition cost data to develop a new, publically available national price benchmark called the National Average Drug Acquisition Cost (NADAC) for Medicaid-covered outpatient prescription drugs.[12] In late 2012, CMS began publishing the resulting NADACs in draft form to help states assess how the use of the NADACs may affect their reimbursements to pharmacies.[13] CMS officials noted that states may choose to modify their drug reimbursement methodologies to use final NADACs by amending their Medicaid state plan.[14]

Because the NADACs are a new source of pharmacy acquisition cost data for states to consider in setting their reimbursements rates, it is important to understand how CMS develops the NADACs. Additionally, given questions about Medicaid FULs with regards to over- and under-reimbursing pharmacies for dispensing outpatient prescription drugs to Medicaid beneficiaries, it is important to understand how PPACA-based FULs compare to pharmacy acquisition costs. Accordingly, you asked us to examine the NADACs and the PPACA-based FUL formula. This report (1) describes how CMS develops the NADACs and (2) examines how PPACA-based FULs compare to the NADACs.

To describe how CMS develops the NADACs, we collected and reviewed CMS documentation on its methodology for calculating the NADACs, which included the process for surveying retail pharmacies, as well as comments stakeholders provided to CMS. We also reviewed NADACs published during the first quarter of 2013. In addition, we interviewed officials from CMS and Myers and Stauffer, LC (hereafter referred to as Myers and Stauffer), a public accounting firm, with which CMS contracted to develop the NADACs.

To examine how PPACA-based FULs compare to NADACs, we compared the PPACA-based FULs to the NADACs for first quarter 2013 in aggregate across all drugs subject to the FUL.[15] To make the aggregate comparison, we first determined a total FUL amount by multiplying each drug's FUL by its Medicaid utilization in the first quarter 2013—the most recent at the time we conducted our analysis—and summing these amounts across all drugs. We then followed a similar process to determine the total NADAC amount for the same drugs. Finally, we compared the total FUL amount to the total NADAC amount to determine the aggregate difference. In addition, we compared the PPACA-based FULs to the NADACs across generic versions and across branded generic versions—brand-name drugs with therapeutically equivalent versions, otherwise known as innovator multiple-source drugs.[16] We also compared the PPACA-based FULs to the NADACs for a subset of the 50 drugs with the highest Medicaid expenditures—accounting for 42 percent of all Medicaid drug expenditures for drugs subject to the FUL—and for the 50 drugs with the highest Medicaid utilization—

accounting for 36 percent of all Medicaid prescriptions for drugs subject to the FUL—in the first quarter of 2013.

To assess the reliability of the NADACs, PPACA-based FULs, and Medicaid utilization data we used, we performed electronic testing for missing and inconsistent data and reviewed documents describing the methodology and quality assurance steps used for collecting and managing the data as well as calculating the NADACs and PPACA-based FULs. We also interviewed agency officials knowledgeable about the data. We determined that the data were sufficiently reliable for the purposes of this report. (See app. I for more details on our methodology.)

We conducted this performance audit from July 2013 through December 2013 in accordance with generally accepted government auditing standards. Those standards require that we plan and perform the audit to obtain sufficient, appropriate evidence to provide a reasonable basis for our findings and conclusions based on our audit objectives. We believe that the evidence obtained provides a reasonable basis for our findings and conclusions based on our audit objectives.

BACKGROUND

Medicaid Coverage of Prescription Drugs

Outpatient prescription drug coverage is an optional benefit that all state Medicaid programs have elected to include in their Medicaid benefit packages. The outpatient prescription drugs covered by Medicaid include brand-name drugs and multiple-source drugs, the latter of which include branded generic versions and generic versions.

State Medicaid programs may use different methods for reimbursing pharmacies for outpatient prescription drugs dispensed to Medicaid beneficiaries. In general, states base their Medicaid reimbursements to a retail pharmacy for a covered outpatient prescription drug on the lowest of the following: a state's best estimate of retail pharmacies' acquisition costs for the drug; the usual and customary charge of the retail pharmacy that dispensed the drug; the state's maximum allowable cost for the drug, if applicable; or the FUL for the drug, if applicable.[17]

Medicaid FULs

Historically, CMS has calculated the FULs by grouping the therapeutically equivalent branded generic and generic versions of drugs, identifying the version with the lowest price published in national drug pricing compendia, and multiplying that price by 150 percent.[18] However, FULs do not apply to branded generic versions if the prescribing provider certifies that the specific brand is medically necessary for a particular patient.[19]

Congress has twice since 2006 enacted legislation that required a change to the FUL formula. Congress's first change to the FUL formula was in the Deficit Reduction Act of 2005 (DRA). Specifically, the DRA required FULs to be calculated as 250 percent of AMP for a drug's least costly therapeutic equivalent.[20] CMS issued a final rule in July 2007 to implement the DRA formula.[21] However, a lawsuit filed by two retail pharmacy industry groups—the National Association of Chain Drug Stores and the National Community Pharmacists Association— challenged the implementation of this rule primarily due to concerns that the revised formula would result in reimbursement well below retail pharmacies' acquisition costs. These concerns were, in part, based on work by GAO and the HHS OIG.[22] In December 2007, the U.S. District Court for the District of Columbia issued a preliminary injunction prohibiting CMS from implementing this final rule to the extent that it affected Medicaid reimbursement rates to retail pharmacies.[23] In July 2008, the Medicare Improvement for Patients and Providers Act of 2008 prohibited CMS from implementing the FUL provisions of the 2007 rule and provided CMS with the authority to issue FULs under the pre-DRA formula through September 2009. Accordingly, CMS stopped calculating and publishing FULs and continued to apply the FULs as calculated at that time.

In March 2010, legislation was again enacted that required a change to the formula for calculating the FUL. Under PPACA, FULs must be calculated as no less than 175 percent of the utilization-based weighted average of the most recent monthly reported AMP for a drug's pharmaceutical and therapeutic equivalents. Because PPACA specified a percentage multiplier for AMP-based FULs of at least 175, in implementing the modified formula the Secretary of HHS has the discretion to increase this percentage multiplier above that level. PPACA also changed the definition of AMP for outpatient prescription drugs and required the Secretary of HHS to implement a process to smooth out fluctuations in the AMPs reported by manufacturers.[24] PPACA also provided that these changes become effective as of October 1, 2010, regardless of whether CMS issued final regulations by that date. Notwithstanding this effective date, CMS has continued to apply the FULs as calculated in 2009 rather than implementing the PPACA-based FULs.[25]

CMS has taken some steps towards addressing the PPACA-based FUL formula, including the issuance of a proposed rule in February 2012.[26] As part of this rule, CMS proposed using the minimum 175 percent multiplier in the calculation of FULs, which the agency determined would result in adequate reimbursement for pharmacies.[27] In calculating the PPACA-based FULs, CMS proposed relying on the designation as a brand-name drug, branded generic version, or generic version from the AMP data reported by manufacturers.[28] In addition, CMS proposed various calculations for smoothing fluctuations in the FULs, such as using the mean of the monthly weighted AMPs for a FUL product group over a specific period of time, as the agency found significant variability in the PPACA-based FULs from month to month. During the comment period for the proposed rule, CMS received a number of comments from a variety of stakeholders, such as independent pharmacy associations, chain drug stores, and drug manufacturers. Many stakeholders that commented on the application of the 175 percent multiplier to the weighted AMP noted the importance of the flexibility provided by PPACA for CMS to increase the 175 percent multiplier in certain circumstances. A number of stakeholders also recommended that CMS implement a smoothing process for the FULs.

In order to provide states with the opportunity to assess reimbursement under the PPACA-based FUL formula before it is implemented, CMS began publishing monthly PPACA-based FULs.[29] Specifically, CMS publishes two sets of PPACA-based FULs. One set, which has been available on a monthly basis since late 2011, is based on AMP data from a single month. In response to stakeholder requests that CMS smooth fluctuations in the single month FULs, a second set of PPACA-based FULs using AMP data from 3 months has also been available on a monthly basis since late 2012. To develop the 3-month rolling average, CMS calculates a weighted average of the most recent and prior 2 months' AMPs. CMS does not calculate this 3-month rolling average for any product group that did not meet the criteria for calculating a single-month FUL in any of the 3 months.[30] This approach could result in some drugs not being subject to FULs that otherwise would be if a single-month FUL were used.

NADAC

To develop the NADACs for outpatient prescription drugs, CMS entered into a contract with Myers and Stauffer to survey retail community pharmacies across the country on their drug acquisition costs. These acquisition costs are to reflect any discounts and rebates pharmacies may receive to the extent available.[31] CMS published a draft methodology of the survey process in May 2012 and began sending surveys to retail community pharmacies beginning in June 2012. CMS also held three webinars between June and December 2012 to provide additional explanation of the draft methodology and receive feedback from stakeholders, such as state Medicaid programs and pharmacy industry groups. Stakeholders provided a range of comments seeking additional clarification and explanation regarding the draft methodology. CMS began publishing NADACs in draft form in late 2012.

CMS Develops NADACs by Surveying Retail Community Pharmacies for Invoice Data on Actual Acquisition Costs

CMS develops NADACs for outpatient prescription drugs by surveying a sample of retail community pharmacies, collecting invoices on actual drug acquisition costs, and calculating NADACs based on the invoice data. Figure 1 summarizes the process CMS follows for developing NADACs.

CMS develops NADACs by performing the following six steps:

1. *Selects a random sample of retail community pharmacies to survey each month.* Each month, CMS selects a simple random sample of approximately 2,500 retail community pharmacies out of more than 60,000 such pharmacies in the US to survey for acquisition cost data.[32] According to CMS officials, this sample is nationally representative because it reflects characteristics of all retail community pharmacies in the US—namely, the proportion of chain and independent pharmacies and the proportion located in urban and rural areas, which can have different acquisition costs.[33] In determining the sample size, CMS and Myers and Stauffer officials considered two main factors: (1) that 400 to 500 pharmacies are needed to respond in order to develop NADACs for most Medicaid

covered prescription drugs and (2) to reach this target, at least 2,000 pharmacies need to be surveyed each month given anticipated response rates from pharmacies based on prior survey experiences. Myers and Stauffer officials also determined that the sample size would limit the burden on pharmacies to respond to the survey since the chances of an individual pharmacy being selected twice in the same year is less than 5 percent.

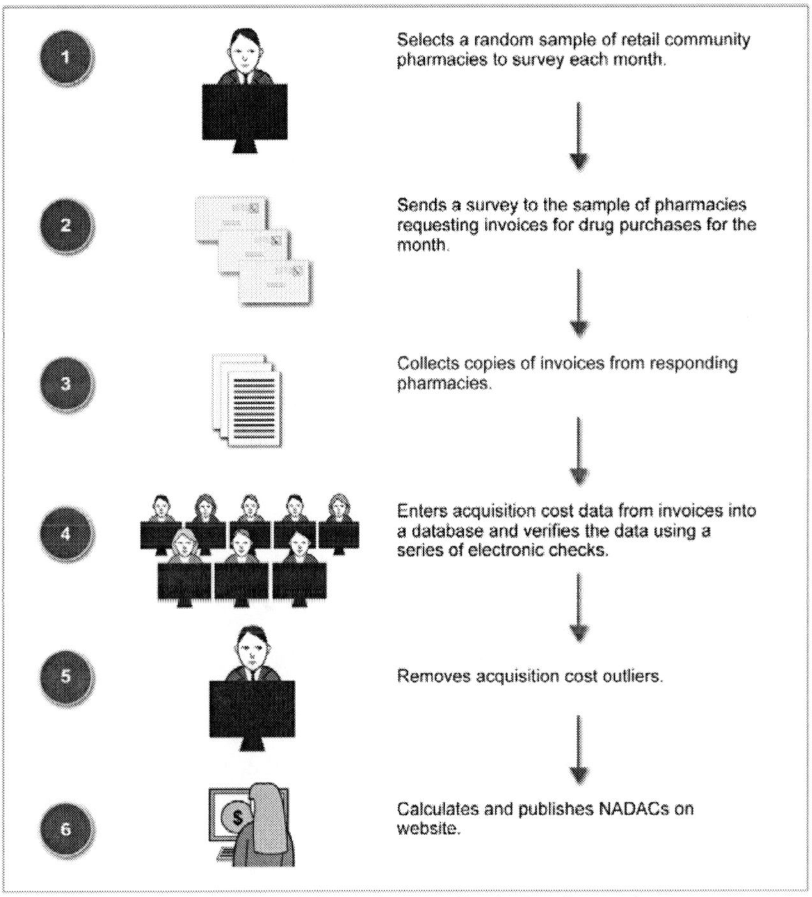

Source: GAO analysis of CMD information; Art Explosion (images).

Figure 1. CMS Process for Acquisition Costs Developing National Average Drug (NADAC) for Outpatient Prescription Drugs.

2. *Sends a survey to the sample of pharmacies requesting invoices for drug purchases.* CMS sends the survey to the sample of pharmacies requesting all invoices for drugs purchased from manufacturers and wholesalers during the reporting month. CMS and Myers and Stauffer officials noted that collecting actual invoices provided more reliable acquisition cost data than having pharmacies manually enter invoice costs into a survey and places a relatively low administrative burden on pharmacies. For each purchase, invoices must provide (1) the 11-digit national drug code (NDC) identifying the product purchased,[34] (2) the price paid, (3) the quantity purchased, and (4) purchase date. CMS and Myers and Stauffer officials indicated one limitation of using invoice data is that the extent to which rebates and discounts from wholesalers and manufacturers are reflected in the "price paid" is currently unknown. These officials also said some rebates and discounts may be included but, based on past experience, may not be significant compared to those occurring off-invoice or those not tied to a specific drug purchase.[35] To address this limitation, CMS is planning to examine off-invoice rebates and discounts more closely. CMS officials stated they plan to use a survey to collect additional information from retail community pharmacies regarding such rebates and discounts in the future.
3. *Collects copies of invoices from responding pharmacies.* According to CMS and Myers and Stauffer officials, approximately 500 to 600 pharmacies respond with invoice data to the monthly surveys. While this number of responses represents about 30 percent of the approximately 2,500 surveyed pharmacies, it meets or exceeds the target of 400 to 500 pharmacies that are needed to develop NADACs for most covered prescription drugs. However, unlike the sample of 2,500 surveyed pharmacies, the proportion of chain and independent pharmacies and the proportion rural and urban pharmacies that respond to the survey do not reflect the proportions of these pharmacies nationally. For example, chain pharmacies typically account for approximately 36 percent of survey responses, but account for about 65 percent of all retail community pharmacies. Similarly, independent pharmacies typically account for approximately 64 percent of survey responses, but account for about 35 percent of all retail community pharmacies.[36] While these differences are a limitation of the survey process, their impact on the NADACs is minimal based on analyses by Myers and Stauffer.[37]

Myers and Stauffer will continue to monitor the proportion of chain and independent pharmacies that respond to the survey compared to the proportion of these pharmacies nationally to ensure acquisition cost data collected reflects national acquisition costs.

4. *Enters acquisition cost data from invoices into a database and verifies the data using a series of electronic and manual checks.* As CMS receives responses from surveyed pharmacies, CMS enters data from the invoices into a database and verifies the data. CMS uses a series of electronic and manual checks to determine whether the invoice data meet several verification criteria: (1) data are from the sampled pharmacies, (2) NDCs are valid and active, (3) purchase dates are from the appropriate month, (4) drug products are on the latest CMS rebate drug product data file,[38] (5) drug products have not been declared less-than-effective by the Drug Efficacy Study Implementation program,[39] (6) only one invoice cost per NDC per pharmacy, and (7) the purchase prices for all drug products reported from an individual pharmacy are not equal to or greater than its average wholesale prices.[40] If any of the criteria are not met, CMS excludes the data from consideration for calculating a drug's NADAC. As a final check, Myers and Stauffer staff manually compare data from the database to the submitted invoices to verify the accuracy and completeness of the data entered.
5. *Removes acquisition cost outliers.* CMS removes any acquisition costs that are outliers. To do this, CMS identifies each drug product as either brand or generic and then groups the brand and generic versions with the same active ingredient(s), strength, dosage form, and route of administration.[41] Within each grouping, CMS reviews the acquisition costs and removes those that are greater than two standard deviations from the mean unit cost of the grouping.
6. *Calculates and publishes NADACs on the CMS website.* CMS calculates NADACs for brand and generic versions once outliers are removed. CMS first calculates a simple average based on the acquisition cost data obtained through the survey. CMS then updates these amounts to reflect changes in the acquisition costs between the time data were collected and the time at which CMS is ready to publish NADACs.[42] CMS updates NADACs for brand versions on a weekly basis to reflect pricing changes in the wholesale acquisition cost (WAC), which are relatively proportional to changes in pharmacy acquisition costs according to CMS officials.[43] For example, if there is

a 5 percent increase in the WAC of a particular brand version, retail community pharmacies' acquisition costs will also increase by 5 percent. By updating the NADACs weekly to reflect this correlation, CMS helps ensure the NADACs for brand versions reflect the most current acquisition costs at the time NADACs are published. Brand and generic versions are also reviewed and adjusted based on research initiated by pharmacy inquiries to the NADAC help desk—a service established to support pharmacies and state Medicaid agencies during the survey process and in response to notifications of drug price changes not reflected in the published NADACs. CMS publishes the updated NADACs on a weekly basis on the Medicaid website.[44] CMS has developed about 5,000 NADACs that relate to more than 22,000 NDCs and that CMS estimated would apply to over 90 percent of drug claims reimbursed by Medicaid.[45]

While CMS and Myers and Stauffer officials acknowledged some limitations exist in developing the NADACs, they also expressed confidence in their current process as one that is both robust and representative of actual acquisition costs. In particular, Myers and Stauffer officials noted that each of the six steps in developing the NADACs included various quality assurance checks. For example, in addition to the systematic procedures for removing acquisition invoice cost outliers, a review team of pharmacists, accountants, and analysts also manually review data for reasonableness. This review may involve evaluating factors that influence drug prices, such as drug shortages and manufacturer price increases.

First Quarter 2013 PPACA-Based FULs Were Nearly Equal to NADACs across All Drugs in Aggregate, but Varied Greatly for Individual Drugs

Using the single-month PPACA-based FULs for all drugs subject to the FUL in the first quarter of 2013, we found the FULs were nearly equal to NADACs for these drugs in aggregate. Specifically, the total of the PPACA-based FUL amount for the 1,035 drugs included in our analysis was about 1.4 percent lower than the total NADAC amount for the same drugs.[46] Individually, PPACA-based FULs for slightly less than half— 508—of the

1,035 drugs were lower than the NADACs for the same drugs. (See figure 2.) Conversely, PPACA-based FULs for slightly more than half—527—of the drugs were higher than the NADACs. PPACA-based FULs for individual drugs ranged from 96 percent lower than to 404 percent higher than the NADACs for the same drugs. In addition, PPACA-based FULs were slightly lower than NADACs for most of the 50 highest expenditure drugs, and nearly the same for most of the 50 highest utilization drugs we reviewed. (See app. II and III for additional details on our analysis comparing PPACA-based FULs and NADACs for the 50 highest expenditure and 50 highest utilization drugs.)

While we found that the PPACA-based FULs for the 1,035 drugs included in our analysis were nearly equally to NADACs in the aggregate, we found large differences for generic and for branded generic versions of these drugs. Specifically, we found that, in the aggregate, the total PPACA-based FUL amount for the generic versions of drugs was 19 percent higher than the total NADAC amount for these same versions. We also found that, in the aggregate, the total PPACA-based FUL amount for the branded generic versions of drugs was 26 percent lower than the total NADAC amount for the same versions. While PPACA-based FULs are published for branded generic and generic versions of drugs, they would not apply to branded generics that are prescribed as medically necessary per CMS's proposed rule. CMS officials stated that in practice, branded generic versions generally are not dispensed unless they are prescribed as medically necessary. However, Medicaid data do not indicate whether dispensed branded generic versions were prescribed as medically necessary and CMS officials noted that the agency is still considering how the PPACA-based FULs will apply to branded generic versions in the final rule.

Comparisons of PPACA-based 3-month rolling average FULs to NADACs resulted in findings that were generally within a few percentage points of the findings using the PPACA-based single-month FULs except for the comparison of branded generic versions. The total of the PPACA-based 3-month rolling average FUL amount for the drugs included in our analysis was about 4.4 percent lower than the total NADAC amount for the same drugs. However, we found that there were 123 drugs that had a single-month FUL but did not have a 3-month rolling average FUL.[47] We also found that, in the aggregate, the total PPACA-based 3-month rolling average FUL amount for the generic versions of these drugs was 23 percent higher than the total NADAC amount for these same versions. Conversely, we found that, in the aggregate, the total PPACA-based 3-month rolling average FUL amount for the branded generic versions of these drugs was 43 percent lower than the total NADAC amount for the same versions. (See app. IV for additional details on our analysis comparing 3-month rolling average PPACA-based FULs and the NADACs.)

CONCLUSION

FULs are intended to control federal Medicaid expenditures on outpatient prescription drugs that are subject to the FUL while ensuring beneficiary access to those drugs. However, CMS has not calculated and published FULs since September 2009 when its authority to use the pre-DRA formula expired. As a result, CMS continues to apply FULs that were calculated more than 4 years ago, a practice that has not ensured effective control of federal reimbursement for the drugs subject to the FUL. In the interim, PPACA modified the FUL formula and established an effective date of October 1, 2010, regardless of whether CMS had issued final regulations. In response, CMS has issued a proposed rule and determined that its proposed implementation of the PPACA-based FUL formula will provide for adequate reimbursement to pharmacies.

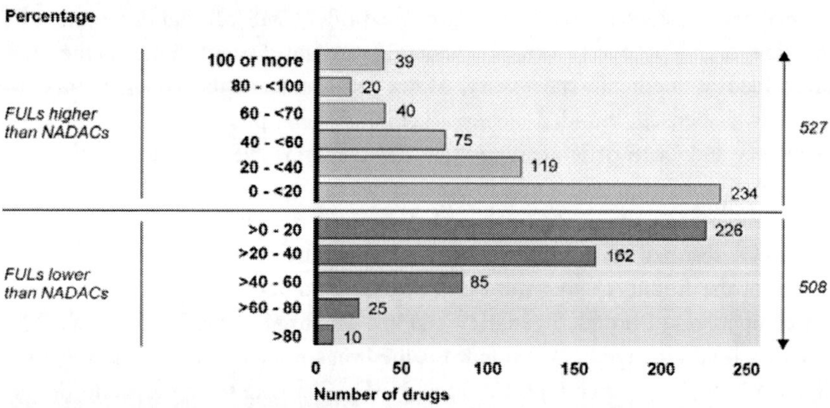

Source: GAO analysis of CMS data.

Figure 2. Comparison of Single-Month PPACA-Based Federal Upper Limits (FUL) to National Average Drug Acquisition Costs (NADAC), First Quarter 2013.

Our work, which found that PPACA-based FULs were nearly equal to the NADACs in the aggregate for all drugs subject to the FUL in first quarter 2013, indicates CMS is close to having a formula under which FULs better reflect pharmacy acquisition costs than they did under past formulas. However, the actual relationship between the PPACA-based FULs and NADACs may be affected by several factors. For example, although the NADAC provides a national benchmark for pharmacy acquisition costs based on invoices reflecting actual drug purchases from 500 to 600 pharmacies, the NADACs may vary from actual acquisition costs experienced among individual pharmacies across the country. Additionally, not all rebates and discounts are reflected on invoices collected during monthly surveys to pharmacies. If they were included, any applicable rebates and discounts would reduce the NADACs calculated by CMS, which would have at least somewhat reduced the slight difference in the PPACA-based FULs and NADACs we identified in first quarter 2013. Given this, we agree with CMS's plans to further study off-invoice rebates and discounts to understand how these may affect NADACs. Further, our analysis—which found that, on average, PPACA-based FULs exceeded NADACs for generic versions but not for branded-generic versions of drugs—indicates that the extent to which PPACA-based FULs will be applied to branded generic versions will also affect the aggregate relationship between the PPACA-based FULs and NADACs. There is also some uncertainty about how PPACA-based FULs and NADACs will compare over time, as our analysis was limited to the first full quarter of the newly published NADACs, the latest available data at the time we conducted our analysis. To determine whether our early findings regarding the relationship between the PPACA-based FULs and the NADACs hold over time will require ongoing monitoring by CMS.

RECOMMENDATION FOR EXECUTIVE ACTION

We recommend the Secretary of HHS direct the Administrator of CMS take the following actions:

- Expeditiously implement the PPACA-based FUL formula to better control federal reimbursement for Medicaid covered outpatient prescription drugs; and
- Monitor the relationship between PPACA-based FULs and the NADACs on an ongoing basis to help determine whether PPACA-based FULs effectively control federal Medicaid expenditures without reducing beneficiary access to drugs subject to FULs over time.

Agency Comments and Our Evaluation

We provided HHS a draft of this report for comments. In its written comments, HHS concurred with our two recommendations and provided other remarks on our findings, as further discussed below.

HHS concurred with our recommendation that CMS expeditiously implement the PPACA-based FUL formula to better control federal reimbursement for Medicaid covered outpatient prescription drugs. HHS stated that CMS announced in late November 2013 that it anticipates implementing the final PPACA-based FULs in July 2014, in order to provide states an opportunity to revise their reimbursement methodologies and adjust their reimbursement payment systems to incorporate the new PPACA-based FULs. HHS also concurred with our recommendation that CMS should monitor the relationship between PPACA-based FULs and the NADACs on an ongoing basis. HHS noted that CMS has been conducting analyses comparing PPACA-based FULs and NADACs and plans to continue these efforts.

HHS also commented on our findings, noting that CMS's analyses examining the relationship between PPACA-based FULs and NADACs found that, in aggregate, FULs were generally higher than NADACs. HHS indicated our inclusion of branded generic versions of drugs subject to the FUL in our analysis does not reflect that FULs typically do not apply to such versions because these versions are rarely dispensed unless prescribed as medically necessary. HHS also noted that our comparison of generic versions of drugs is consistent with HHS's analysis showing that the PPACA-based FULs were generally higher than NADACs. As we stated in our draft report, Medicaid data do not indicate whether dispensed branded generic versions were prescribed as medically necessary and thus do not identify specifically which dispensed branded generic versions would be subject to FULs. Further, in our discussion with CMS officials, they noted that the agency was still considering how the PPACA-based FULs would apply to branded generic versions in the final rule. Given this, we believe that our inclusion of branded generic versions is a more conservative approach to examining the relationship between the PPACA-based FULs and NADACs than entirely excluding these versions. We also reported information that separately analyzed PPACA-based FULs and NADACs for generic versions and branded generic versions. In its comments, HHS also noted that CMS finalized the NADACs in late November 2013 and suggested that states may want to consider using the NADACs as part of their reimbursement methodology.

HHS also provided technical comments, which we incorporated as appropriate.

John E. Dicken
Director, Health Care

APPENDIX I. METHODOLOGY FOR COMPARING FEDERAL UPPER LIMITS TO NATIONAL AVERAGE DRUG ACQUISITION COSTS

To examine how the Patient Protection and Affordable Care Act (PPACA)-based Medicaid Federal Upper Limits (FUL) compared to National Average Drug Acquisition Costs (NADAC), we compared first quarter 2013 PPACA-based FULs to NADACs both in aggregate and individually for (1) all drugs subject to the FUL, (2) branded generic

versions of drugs subject to the FUL, (3) generic versions of drugs subject to the FUL, (4) a subset of the 50 highest expenditure drugs based on Medicaid reimbursement, and (5) a subset the 50 highest utilization drugs based on Medicaid prescriptions filled.

To conduct our analyses we used three data sources from CMS:

- **Draft PPACA-based FULs**: we examined PPACA-based single-month FULs for first quarter 2013.[48] We calculated a quarterly FUL price for each drug by taking the simple average of the 3 monthly FULs for that quarter. For purposes of this report, we consider a drug to consist of all the National Drug Codes (NDC) within a single FUL group.[49]
- **Draft NADACs**: for each of the drugs with a single-month FUL, we examined the corresponding NADACs published for first quarter 2013.[50] We calculated a quarterly NADAC price for each drug by taking a simple average of the weekly NADACs.
- **Medicaid Drug Utilization Data**: to examine how the single-month FULs compared to NADACs in aggregate across all drugs included in our analyses, we used national Medicaid utilization data from first quarter 2013, which included both fee-for-service and managed care data, to weight our analyses. We also used this data to select the 50 highest expenditure drugs—accounting for 42 percent of all Medicaid

expenditures for drugs covered by the FUL—and the 50 highest utilization drugs—accounting for 36 percent of all Medicaid prescriptions for drugs covered by the FUL. This utilization data was the latest available at the time of our analysis.

To compare the FULs to the NADACs in the aggregate, we (1) multiplied the FUL for each drug by its utilization and then summed all the FULs across the drugs, (2) multiplied the NADAC for each drug by its utilization and then summed all the NADACs across the drugs, and (3) compared the sum of the FULs to the sum of the NADACs. We repeated these same steps to examine how 3-month rolling average FULs compared to NADACs for first quarter 2013 in the aggregate.[51]

We also conducted additional analyses to test the sensitivity of our results for first quarter 2013. Specifically, (1) to determine the extent to which there may be month-to-month variation in our results, we reviewed how single-month FULs compared to NADACs for each month in first quarter 2013 and (2) since CMS typically does not publish the FULs until about 2 months after the actual manufacturer sales on which it is based have occurred, we compared single-month FULs that would have been available for states to use to reimburse pharmacies in first quarter 2013 if CMS had published FULs in final form on its website to NADACs.[52] The results of our sensitivity analyses were about the same as the results of our original analysis.

We reviewed all data for soundness and consistency and determined that they were sufficiently reliable for our purposes. Specifically, we performed electronic testing for missing and inconsistent data, reviewed CMS documents on the data, and spoke with CMS officials knowledgeable about the data. To test for missing and inconsistent data, we used 11 digit NDCs to identify a drug in our three data sources.

We only included those NDCs in our analyses that had a published FUL in any month of first quarter 2013, a published NADAC in any month of first quarter 2013, and had utilization data for first quarter 2013. While there were 1,060 drugs with a single-month FUL in first quarter 2013, we dropped 25 drugs from our analyses because of a lack of NADAC data.[53] We also excluded those NDCs that did not meet all the criteria for having a FUL, including those NDCs for which CMS listed a FUL for a single source drug and that were not rated as being fully therapeutically equivalent.[54] We also excluded NDCs that listed different unit types across the FUL and NADAC data sets.

We reviewed CMS documentation describing the methodology used to generate the data and the quality assurance steps that were followed for each data set. We also discussed the data with knowledgeable officials from CMS—specifically, we discussed the steps to collect and process the data, any limitations on the data's accuracy and completeness, and steps CMS takes to assure data quality.

There are limitations to our comparison of FULs to NADACs. We examined data representing only one quarter of 2013, which may not be representative of the relationship between FULs and NADAC for other months or quarters of that year or future years. Additionally, the extent to which off-invoice rebates and discounts are captured in the NADAC calculation is also a limitation and could lower the NADACs used in our analyses. Finally, all data used in this analysis are national and may not represent the experience of individual pharmacies and states across the country.

APPENDIX II. COMPARISON OF FEDERAL UPPER LIMITS TO NATIONAL AVERAGE DRUG ACQUISITION COSTS, TOP 50 MEDICAID EXPENDITURE DRUGS

We compared the Patient Protection and Affordable Care Act (PPACA)-based single-month Federal Upper Limits (FUL) to the National Average Drug Acquisition Costs (NADAC) for the first quarter of 2013 for the 50 highest expenditure drugs subject to the FUL based on Medicaid reimbursement in first quarter 2013. In the aggregate, the total PPACA-based FUL amount for the 50 highest expenditure drugs was 5 percent lower than the total NADAC amount for the same drugs.

We also found that 41 of the 50 highest expenditure drugs included branded-generic versions. Among the 50 highest expenditure drugs, PPACA-based FULs ranged from 69 percent lower to 64 percent higher than NADACs and 29 drugs had PPACA-based FULs lower than NADACs. Table 1 below summarizes the results of our comparisons for these high expenditure drugs.

Table 1. Comparison of Single-Month PPACA-Based Federal Upper Limits (FUL) to National Average Drug Acquisition Costs (NADAC) for the 50 Highest Medicaid Expenditure Drugs Subject to the FUL

Drug name and strength (dosage form)	Total number of Medicaid prescriptions	Total Medicaid reimbursement[a]	Percent that FUL is higher than (or lower than) NADAC	FUL group includes-branded-generic versions[b]
Methylphenidate hydrochloride 36mg (extended release tablet)	296,096	$58,205,864	27.8%	Yes
Amphetamine aspartate; amphetamine sulfate; dextroamphetamine saccharate; dextroamphetamine sulfate 20mg (extended release capsule)	192,336	$42,655,407	(0.3%)	Yes
Methylphenidate hydrochloride 54mg (extended release tablet)	219,753	$38,812,213	28.1%	Yes
Amphetamine aspartate; amphetamine sulfate; dextroamphetamine saccharate; dextroamphetamine sulfate 30mg (extended release capsule)	165,996	$34,603,783	19.2%	Yes
Cefdinir 250mg/5ml (suspension)	349,245	$24,577,411	(54.2%)	No
Methylphenidate hydrochloride 27mg (extended release tablet)	148,954	$23,129,472	16.2%	Yes
Ziprasidone hydrochloride 80mg (capsule)	80,214	$23,077,344	(15.6%)	Yes
Amphetamine aspartate; amphetamine sulfate; dextroamphetamine saccharate; dextroamphetamine sulfate 10mg (extended release capsule)	119,591	$22,376,497	(3.9%)	Yes
Olanzapine 20mg (tablet)	74,736	$22,288,978	(43.9%)	Yes
Quetiapine fumarate 300mg(tablet)	122,409	$19,891,900	(50.9%)	Yes
Amphetamine aspartate; amphetamine sulfate; dextroamphetamine saccharate; dextroamphetamine sulfate 15 mg (extended release capsule)	97,754	$18,085,246	7.5%	Yes

Drug name and strength (dosage form)	Total number of Medicaid prescriptions	Total Medicaid reimbursement[a]	Percent that FUL is higher than (or lower than) NADAC	FUL group includes-branded-generic versions[b]
Quetiapine fumarate 200mg (tablet)	138,133	$17,858,754	(49.5%)	Yes
Azithromycin 200mg/5ml (suspension)	798,759	$17,131,334	(16.8%)	Yes
Tacrolimus 1mg (capsule)	57,113	$17,117,891	20.0%	Yes
Quetiapine fumarate 400mg (tablet)	86,733	$15,882,157	(46.0%)	Yes
Montelukast sodium 5mg (chewable tablet)	438,743	$15,619,948	10.7%	Yes
Olanzapine 10mg (tablet)	83,794	$15,282,033	(50.1%)	Yes
Amoxicillin 400mg/5ml (suspension)	1,540,964	$14,321,528	(19.9%)	Yes
Olanzapine 15mg (tablet)	50,948	$13,643,832	(46.5%)	Yes
Acetaminophen; oxycodone hydrochloride 325mg; 10mg (tablet)	289,423	$13,456,537	20.3%	No
Amphetamine aspartate; amphetamine sulfate; dextroamphetamine saccharate; dextroamphetamine sulfate 25mg (extended release capsule)	65,484	$13,195,339	(5.1%)	Yes
Omeprazole 20mg (delayed release capsule)	1,169,782	$13,168,847	28.8%	Yes
Divalproex sodium 500mg (extended release tablet)	247,355	$13,043,598	28.4%	Yes
Quetiapine fumarate 100mg (tablet)	187,744	$12,682,377	(57.5%)	Yes
Azithromycin 250mg (tablet)	1,223,048	$12,513,992	(22.3%)	Yes
Clopidogrel Bisulfate 75mg (tablet)	357,703	$12,272,079	2.6%	Yes
Acetaminophen; hydrocodone bitartrate 325mg; 10mg (tablet)	460,950	$10,836,338	(24.4%)	No
Ziprasidone hydrochloride 60mg (capsule)	39,987	$10,487,768	(18.8%)	Yes

Table 1. (Continued)

Drug name and strength (dosage form)	Total number of Medicaid prescriptions	Total Medicaid reimbursement[a]	Percent that FUL is higher than (or lower than) NADAC	FUL group includes-branded-generic versions[b]
Permethrin 5% (cream)	191,998	$10,427,828	1.8%	No
Omeprazole 40mg (delayed release capsule)	563,859	$10,234,185	14.5%	Yes
Escitalopram oxalate 20mg (tablet)	226,560	$10,093,613	(30.8%)	Yes
Lamivudine; zidovudine 150mg; 300mg (tablet)	13,997	$10,031,093	53.8%	Yes
Pioglitazone hydrochloride 30 mg (tablet)	47,405	$9,888,358	(67.3%)	Yes
Polyethylene glycol 3350 17gm (powder)	442,756	$9,812,873	11.1%	No
Valacyclovir hydrochloride 500mg (tablet)	114,470	$9,481,547	(40.4%)	Yes
Oxycodone hydrochloride 30mg (tablet)	151,142	$9,471,666	1.9%	No
Amoxicillin; clavulanic acid 875mg; 125mg (tablet)	382,380	$9,316,296	(38.7%)	Yes
Modafinil 200 mg (tablet)	9,964	$9,309,238	(25.4%)	Yes
Gabapentin 300mg (capsule)	627,146	$9,219,813	40.9%	Yes
Clozapine 100mg (tablet)	72,320	$9,137,289	47.0%	Yes
Ziprasidone hydrochloride 40mg (capsule)	45,734	$9,125,666	(18.7%)	Yes
Cefdinir 125mg/5ml (suspension)	210,063	$9,021,313	(41.0%)	No
Fentanyl 100mcg (film)	25,415	$9,020,333	28.4%	Yes
Montelukast sodium 4 mg (chewable tablet)	253,879	$9,013,163	6.5%	No
Amphetamine aspartate; amphetamine sulfate; dextroamphetamine saccharate; dextroamphetamine sulfate 20 mg (tablet)	119,141	$8,255,920	(24.9%)	Yes
Pioglitazone hydrochloride 45mg (tablet)	34,830	$7,967,823	(68.9%)	Yes

Drug name and strength (dosage form)	Total number of Medicaid prescriptions	Total Medicaid reimbursement[a]	Percent that FUL is higher than (or lower than) NADAC	FUL group includes-branded-generic versions[b]
Desmopressin acetate 0.2mg (tablet)	79,371	$7,805,000	(33.5%)	Yes
Valacyclovir hydrochloride 1gm (tablet)	77,215	$7,780,332	(38.5%)	Yes
Escitalopram oxalate 10mg (tablet)	171,992	$7,719,647	(48.4%)	Yes
Atorvastatin calcium 20mg (tablet)	192,973	$7,661,997	64.3%	Yes
Total	**13,158,357**	**$766,013,460**		
Total for all Medicaid drugs subject to the FUL[c]	**70,934,358**	**$1,754,665,444**		

Source: GAO analysis of CMS data.

[a] Total Medicaid reimbursement includes amounts states pay to pharmacies using their own methodologies.

[b] Branded-generic versions are brand-name drugs with therapeutically equivalent generic versions.

[c] This is the total for the 1,035 drugs with both FULs and NADACs in first quarter 2013.

APPENDIX III. COMPARISON OF FEDERAL UPPER LIMITS TO NATIONAL AVERAGE DRUG ACQUISITION COSTS, TOP 50 MEDICAID UTILIZATION DRUGS

We compared the Patient Protection and Affordable Care Act (PPACA)-based single-month Federal Upper Limits (FUL) to National Average Drug Acquisition Costs (NADAC) for the first quarter of 2013 for the 50 highest utilization drugs subject to the FUL based on the number of Medicaid prescriptions filled in first quarter 2013. In the aggregate, the total

PPACA-based FUL amount for the 50 highest utilization drugs was 1.8 percent lower than the total NADAC amount for the same drugs. We also found that 31 of the 50 highest utilization drugs included branded-generic versions. Among the 50 highest utilization drugs, PPACA-based FULs ranged from 54 percent lower to 258 percent higher than NADACs and 31 drugs had PPACA-based FULs higher than NADACs. Table 2 below summarizes the results of our comparisons for these high utilization drugs.

Table 2. Comparison of Single-Month PPACA-Based Federal Upper Limits (FUL) to National Average Drug Acquisition Costs (NADAC) for the 50 Highest Medicaid Utilization Drugs Subject to the FUL

Drug name and strength (dosage form)	Total number of Medicaid prescriptions	Total Medicaid reimbursement[a]	Percent that FUL is higher than (or lower than) NADAC	FUL group includes branded-generic versions[b]
Amoxicillin 400mg/5ml (suspension)	1,540,964	$14,321,528	(19.9%)	Yes
Azithromycin 250mg (tablet)	1,223,048	$12,513,992	(22.3%)	Yes
Omeprazole 20mg (delayed release capsule)	1,169,782	$13,168,847	28.8%	Yes
Tramadol hydrochloride 50mg (tablet)	1,056,066	$7,415,078	116.9%	Yes
Ergocalciferol 50000iu (capsule)	915,435	$4,932,530	(18.0%)	Yes
Acetaminophen; hydrocodone bitartate 500mg; 5mg (tablet)	893,728	$5,575,897	(1.1%)	No
Ibuprofen 800mg (tablet)	868,270	$4,749,196	12.7%	No
Amoxicillin 500mg (capsule)	827,419	$4,751,523	(11.5%)	No
Azithromycin 200mg/5ml (suspension)	798,759	$17,131,334	(16.8%)	Yes
Acetaminophen; oxycodone hydrochloride 325mg; 5mg (tablet)	780,009	$6,429,739	124.7%	No
Ibuprofen 600mg (tablet)	706,099	$3,276,242	(3.0%)	No
Folic acid 1mg (tablet)	662,268	$3,028,028	(26.8%)	No
Amoxicillin 250mg/5ml (suspension)	646,289	$5,112,039	(19.6%)	No

Drug name and strength (dosage form)	Total number of Medicaid prescriptions	Total Medicaid reimbursement[a]	Percent that FUL is higher than (or lower than) NADAC	FUL group includes branded-generic versions[b]
Ibuprofen 100mg/5ml (suspension)	640,338	$6,214,432	6.1%	Yes
Gabapentin 300mg (capsule)	627,146	$9,219,813	40.9%	Yes
Zolpidem tartrate 10mg (tablet)	613,169	$3,115,853	205.8%	Yes
Amlodipine besylate 10mg (tablet)	591,798	$3,417,952	38.4%	Yes
Simvastatin 20mg (tablet)	584,065	$3,878,650	258.4%	Yes
Hydrochlorothiazide 25mg (tablet)	584,039	$1,885,987	(25.5%)	No
Clonidine hydrochloride 0.1mg (tablet)	579,656	$3,752,068	7.0%	Yes
Omeprazole 40mg (delayed release capsule)	563,859	$10,234,185	14.5%	Yes
Sertraline hydrochloride 100mg (tablet)	515,116	$4,436,743	59.5%	Yes
Alprazolam 1mg (tablet)	499,203	$3,808,778	59.2%	Yes
Clonazepam 1mg (tablet)	489,458	$3,508,070	31.5%	Yes
Acetaminophen; hydrocodone bitartate 325mg; 10mg (tablet)	460,950	$10,836,338	(24.4%)	No
Lisinopril 20mg (tablet)	459,499	$2,510,837	14.1%	Yes
Amlodipine besylate 5mg (tablet)	458,272	$2,524,117	56.2%	Yes
Lisinopril 10mg (tablet)	455,919	$2,173,460	2.3%	Yes
Citalopram hydrobromide 20mg (tablet)	454,701	$2,635,369	62.5%	Yes
Simvastatin 40mg (tablet)	453,681	$3,346,908	134.7%	Yes
Clonazepam 0.5mg (tablet)	450,300	$2,720,148	76.2%	Yes
Fluoxetine hydrochloride 20mg (capsule)	446,655	$3,066,156	179.4%	Yes
Polyethylene glycol 3350 17gm (powder)	442,756	$9,812,873	11.1%	No

Table 2. (Continued)

Drug name and strength (dosage form)	Total number of Medicaid prescriptions	Total Medicaid reimbursement[a]	Percent that FUL is higher than (or lower than) NADAC	FUL group includes branded-generic versions[b]
Montelukast sodium 5 mg (chewable tablet)	438,743	$15,619,948	10.7%	Yes
Trazodone hydrochloride 50mg (tablet)	420,164	$2,161,362	(0.3%)	No
Sertraline hydrochloride 50mg (tablet)	403,083	$2,880,428	34.1%	Yes
Cephalexin 500mg (capsule)	401,844	$3,053,676	(19.6%)	Yes
Trazodone hydrochloride 100mg (tablet)	393,268	$2,412,039	13.6%	No
Amoxicillin; clavulanic acid 875mg; 125mg (tablet)	382,380	$9,316,296	(38.7%)	Yes
Prednisone 20mg (tablet)	378,602	$1,794,632	38.5%	No
Metronidazole 500mg (tablet)	376,128	$3,569,294	(45.0%)	Yes
Alprazolam 0.5mg (tablet)	376,042	$2,358,658	51.7%	Yes
Promethazine hydrochloride 25mg (tablet)	375,489	$3,102,305	(43.4%)	No
Acetaminophen; codeine phosphate 300mg;30mg (tablet)	365,345	$2,526,844	(25.0%)	No
Clopidogrel bisulfate 75mg (tablet)	357,703	$12,272,079	2.6%	Yes
Cefdinir 250mg/5ml (suspension)	349,245	$24,577,411	(54.2%)	No
Dextromethorphan hydro-bromide; promethazine hydrocholoride 15mg/5ml; 6.25mg/5ml (syrup)	339,225	$2,414,183	36.5%	No
Pantoprazole sodium 40mg (delayed release tablet)	328,358	$4,896,464	107.1%	Yes
Citalopram hydrobromide 40mg (tablet)	327,904	$1,879,229	59.2%	Yes

Drug name and strength (dosage form)	Total number of Medicaid prescriptions	Total Medicaid reimbursement[a]	Percent that FUL is higher than (or lower than) NADAC	FUL group includes branded-generic versions[b]
Prednisolone 15mg/5ml (syrup)	318,911	$2,256,691	(1.4%)	No
Total	**28,791,115**	**$292,596,249**		
Total for all Medicaid drugs subject to the FUL[c]	**70,943,358**	**$1,754,665,444**		

Source: GAO analysis of CMS data.

[a] Total Medicaid reimbursement includes amounts states pay to pharmacies using their own methodologies.

[b] Branded-generic versions are brand-name drugs with therapeutically equivalent generic versions.

[c] This is the total for the 1,035 drugs with FULs and NADACs in 2013.

APPENDIX IV. 3-MONTH ROLLING AVERAGE FEDERAL UPPER LIMITS COMPARED WITH NATIONAL AVERAGE DRUG ACQUISITION COSTS

We found that, in aggregate, the total Patient Protection and Affordable Care Act (PPACA)-based 3-month rolling average Federal Upper Limit (FUL) amount was 4.4 percent lower than the total National Average Drug Acquisition Costs (NADAC) amount for 912 drugs included in our analysis.[55] We found that PPACA-based 3-month rolling average FULs were higher than the NADACs for 459 drugs and lower than the NADACs for 453 drugs. Figure 3 shows the number of drugs with 3-month rolling average PPACA-based FULs higher and lower than NADACs for the same drugs.

PPACA-based 3-month rolling average FULs were lower than NADACs for most of the 50 highest expenditure drugs, but higher for most of the 50 highest utilization drugs we reviewed. In the aggregate, the total PPACA-based 3-month rolling average FUL amount for the 50 highest expenditure drugs was 0.6 percent higher than the total NADAC amount for the same drugs. Among the 50 highest expenditure drugs, PPACA-based 3-month rolling average FULs ranged from 40 percent lower to 113 percent higher than NADACs and 29 drugs had PPACA-based FULs lower than the NADACs. Our analysis of the 50 highest utilization drugs found that, in the aggregate, the total PPACA-based FUL amount was 6.2 percent higher than the total NADAC amount for the same drugs. Among the 50 highest utilization drugs, PPACA-based 3-month rolling average FULs ranged from 47 percent lower to 122 percent higher than NADACs and 31 drugs had FULs higher than NADACs.

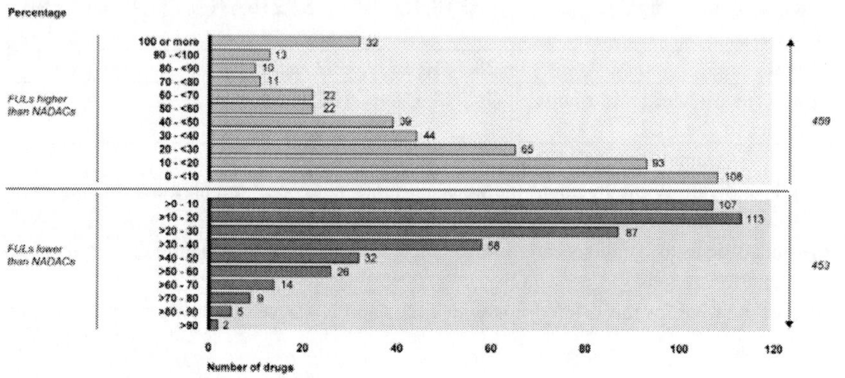

Source: GAO analysis of CMS data.

Figure 3. Comparison of PPACA-Based 3-Month Rolling Average Federal Upper Limits (FUL) to National Average Drug Acquisition Costs (NADAC), First Quarter 2013.

End Notes

[1] The federal government matches most Medicaid expenditures on the basis of a statutory formula known as the Federal Medical Assistance Percentage (FMAP). The FMAP is calculated based on each state's per capita income (PCI) in relation to the national PCI. For fiscal year 2013, states' FMAPs ranged from 50 to 73 percent.

[2] Therapeutically equivalent drugs are defined as those that can be substituted for one another with the full expectation that they will produce the same clinical effect and safety profile as each other. Pharmaceutically equivalent drugs must contain the same active ingredient(s) in the same dosage form and meet strength and other applicable standards.

[3] Each state administers its Medicaid program in accordance with a state Medicaid plan. These plans include methods used to reimburse pharmacies for outpatient prescription drugs.

[4] This aggregate is determined by first multiplying the FUL by the number of units dispensed for each drug in a given state for a given year. The resulting dollar amounts are then added across all drugs subject to a FUL and the sum total represents the maximum amount eligible

for federal matching funds. Therefore, it might be possible for a state Medicaid program to reimburse pharmacies at an amount above the FUL for certain drugs and not exceed the sum of FULs in aggregate if it also reimburses them at an amount below the FUL for other drugs.

[5] These prices are published in three national drug pricing compendia—First DataBank, Medi-Span, and Red Book. According to agency officials, CMS's legal authority to calculate FULs using this formula expired in September 2009. Accordingly, CMS currently continues to apply the FULs that were calculated and published as of September 2009.

[6] Retail pharmacies acquire prescription drugs from manufacturers and drug wholesalers. The price a retail pharmacy pays to these entities is known as a pharmacy's acquisition cost. Drug wholesalers (hereafter referred to as wholesalers) purchase bulk quantities of drugs from pharmaceutical manufacturers and then distribute them to pharmacies.

[7] See HHS OIG, *Medicaid Drug Price Comparisons: Average Manufacturer Price to Published Prices* (Washington, D.C.: June 2005). More recently, the HHS OIG has found that FULs based on national compendia prices were more than four times higher than actual pharmacy acquisition costs. See HHS OIG, *A Comparison of Medicaid Federal Upper Limit Amounts to Acquisition Costs, Medicare Payment Amounts, and Retail Prices* (Washington D.C.: August 2009) and *Analyzing Changes to Medicaid Federal Upper Limit Amounts* (Washington D.C.: October 2012).

[8] Deficit Reduction Act of 2005, Pub. L. No. 109-171, § 6001(a)(2), 120 Stat. 4, 54-55 (2006).

[9] See GAO, *Medicaid Outpatient Drugs: Estimated 2007 Federal Upper Limits for Reimbursement Compared with Retail Pharmacy Acquisition Costs*, GAO-07-239R (Washington, D.C.: Dec. 22, 2006), and HHS OIG, *Deficit Reduction Act of 2005: Impact on the Medicaid Federal Upper Limit Program*, (Washington, D.C.: June 2007).

[10] Specifically, the revised formula uses the weighted average of the most recently reported monthly AMPs for pharmaceutically and therapeutically equivalent multiple-source drugs that are available for purchase by retail community pharmacies on a nationwide basis. Pub. L. No. 111-148, § 2503(a), 124 Stat. 119, 310-312 (2010), as amended by the Health Care and Education Reconciliation Act of 2010 (HCERA), Pub. L. No. 111-152, § 1101(c), 124 Stat. 1029, 1039, and Pub. L. No. 111-226, § 202, 124 Stat. 2389, 2394 (2010). For purposes of this report, references to PPACA include the amendments made by HCERA and Public Law No. 111-226.

[11] Throughout this report, references to PPACA-based FULs refer to FULs based on the PPACA FUL formula, but which are published in draft form. CMS publishes the PPACA-based FULs on a monthly basis on the federal Medicaid website. See http://www.medicaid.gov/Medicaid-CHIP-Program-Information/By-Topics/Benefits/Prescription-Drugs/Federal-Upper-Limits.html, accessed June 18, 2013.

[12] A retail community pharmacy is defined as a pharmacy that is licensed by a state and that dispenses medications to the general public at retail prices. The definition does not include pharmacies that dispense prescription medications to patients primarily through the mail, nursing home pharmacies, hospital pharmacies, and pharmacy benefit managers, among others.

[13] Throughout this report, references to NADACs refer to NADACs published in draft form unless noted otherwise. CMS publishes the NADACs on a weekly basis on the federal Medicaid website. See http://www.medicaid.gov/Medicaid-CHIP-Program-Information/By-Topics/Benefits/Prescription-Drugs/Survey-of-Retail-Prices.html, accessed June 18, 2013.

[14] Any changes to reimbursement methodologies for outpatient prescription drugs generally require CMS review and approval of an amendment to the state plan.

[15] Drugs subject to the FUL accounted for more than $1.75 billion of Medicaid expenditures on outpatient prescription drugs in the first quarter 2013.

[16] In reporting AMP data to CMS for calculating the PPACA-based FULs, manufacturers designate each drug version as single-source, innovator multiple-source, or non-innovator multiple-source. A single-source drug is defined as a brand-name drug with no generic

versions. A brand-name drug is a drug marketed under a proprietary, trademark-protected name. After any patent and market exclusivity for the brand-name drug expires, other drug companies may develop a therapeutic equivalent—generic—version. An innovator multiple-source is defined as a brand-name drug that has available generic versions. A non-innovator multiple-source drug is defined as a generic version. For purposes of this report, we refer to single-source drugs as brand-name drugs, innovator multiple-source drugs as branded generic versions, and non-innovator multiple-source drugs as generic versions.

[17] The usual and customary charge for a drug is the full retail price that individuals without prescription drug coverage pay when purchasing drugs at a retail pharmacy. States that administer a maximum allowable cost program publish lists of selected drugs with the maximum prices at which the state will reimburse for those medications, which are often lower than the FUL for the same drugs. Pharmacies generally do not receive payments that are higher than the state-determined maximum allowable cost.

[18] Published prices included the average wholesale price, wholesale acquisition cost, and direct price. Average wholesale price is the average of the list prices that the manufacturer suggests wholesalers charge pharmacies. Wholesale acquisition cost is the manufacturer's list price for wholesalers or other direct purchasers before any rebates, discounts, allowances, or other price concessions. Direct price as published by First DataBank represents the manufacturer's published catalog or list price for a drug product to nonwholesalers.

[19] In this circumstance, the FUL does not apply and the state may use an alternative payment methodology for that branded generic version.

[20] Pub. L. No. 109-171, § 6001(a)(2), 120 Stat. 4, 54-55 (2006).

[21] 72 Fed. Reg. 39142 (July 17, 2007). The final rule provided that federal reimbursement for drugs subject to a FUL could not exceed, in the aggregate, a reasonable dispensing fee plus an amount established by CMS in accordance with the revised FUL formula. The final rule also provided instructions for drug manufacturers in calculating and reporting AMPs, among other things.

[22] In a 2006 report, we found that, for a sample of 77 drugs, the estimated AMP-based FULs using the DRA formula were on average 36 percent lower than average retail pharmacy acquisition costs for the first quarter of 2006. See GAO-07-239R. In a 2007 report, HHS OIG determined that, on average, pharmacies would have been able to purchase only 6 of 25 selected high-expenditure drugs for less than the AMP-based FULs using the DRA formula during the second quarter of 2006. See HHS OIG, *Deficit Reduction Act of 2005: Impact on the Medicaid Federal Upper Limit Program* (Philadelphia, Pa.: June 2007).

[23] See *National Ass'n of Chain Drug Stores v. Health and Human Servs.*, 631 F. Supp. 2d 17 (D. D.C. 2009).

[24] Among other changes, PPACA specified that AMPs will be the average of prices paid to manufacturers for drugs available for purchase at retail community pharmacies on a nationwide basis. PPACA required the Secretary of HHS to implement a smoothing process for AMPs that is similar to the smoothing process used in determining average sales price of a drug or biologic covered under Medicare Part B. Medicare Part B covers certain physician, outpatient hospital, laboratory and other services, and medical equipment and supplies. Drugs obtained under Medicare Part B are those that are commonly administered by a physician or under a physician's close supervision in physicians' offices and hospital outpatient departments.

[25] In an August 2013 report, the HHS OIG found that had the PPACA-based FUL amounts been implemented in January 2012 the aggregate reimbursement under the PPACA-based FULs would have been 22 percent lower than the aggregate reimbursement under the compendia-based FULs for 32 states. See HHS OIG, *Medicaid Drug Pricing in State Maximum Allowable Cost Programs* (Washington, D.C.: August 2013).

[26] 77 Fed. Reg. 5318 (Feb. 2, 2012).

[27] In a 2010 report, we found that across 40 drugs FULs calculated based on the PPACA formula using the minimum 175 percent multiplier were 78 percent lower than FULs calculated based on compendia prices, but were still 35 percent higher than pharmacy acquisition costs, in the aggregate. See GAO, *Medicaid Outpatient Prescription Drugs: Estimated Changes to Federal Upper Limits Using the Formula under the Patient Protection and Affordable Care Act*, GAO-11-141R (Washington, D.C.: Dec. 15, 2010). Similarly, in a 2012 report, the HHS OIG found that FUL amounts based on the PPACA formula using a 175 percent multiplier were 61 percent lower than FULs based on compendia prices, at the median, and 43 percent higher than pharmacy acquisition costs, in the aggregate. See HHS OIG, *Analyzing Changes to Medicaid Federal Upper Limit Amounts* (Washington D.C.: October 2012).

[28] CMS proposed excluding brand-name drugs from the FUL calculation because statutory provisions require the agency to only use multiple-source drugs in this calculation.

[29] According to CMS officials, the agency typically does not publish the PPACA-based FULs until about 2 months after the actual manufacturer sales on which the FULs are based have occurred. CMS officials indicated that this delay is due in part to the additional 30 days after the end of the month in which sales occurred that manufacturers have to report AMP data. For example, AMP data based on April manufacturer sales would be due to CMS by May 30 and then typically published in June.

[30] Criteria for calculating a FUL for a product group include, among others, having three or more suppliers, having three or more therapeutic equivalents, and having all labelers report and certify an AMP.

[31] Retail community pharmacies can receive discounts and rebates from manufacturers and wholesalers which sell drugs to retail pharmacies.

[32] Data from the National Council for Prescription Drug Programs (NCPDP) are used to identify the universe of retail community pharmacies to sample. According to CMS and Myers and Stauffer officials, the NCPDP data provides the most comprehensive and up-to-date listing of retail community pharmacies.

[33] A chain pharmacy is generally defined as a pharmacy that belongs to a group of four or more pharmacies that are all under the same ownership. There are various definitions of independent pharmacies. In this report, we use the definition from the NCPDP, which defines an independent pharmacy as one to three pharmacies under common ownership.

[34] An NDC is a unique identifying prescription drug product number that is assigned in part by the Food and Drug Administration and registered and listed with it.

[35] Rebates and discounts for retail community pharmacies can occur on a wholesaler's or manufacturer's entire line of products, rather than on a per-drug product basis, and the amounts of rebates and discounts may vary based on retail community pharmacies' negotiations with these entities.

[36] Urban pharmacies account for approximately 68 percent of survey responses but account for 77 percent of all retail community pharmacies. Rural pharmacies typically account for approximately 32 percent of survey responses but account for about 23 percent of all retail community pharmacies.

[37] Myers and Stauffer found that for chain pharmacies the average acquisition costs for generic versions were 1 to 2 percent lower, and for brand versions were about 1 percent higher, than costs for independent pharmacies. Myers and Stauffer also found that for rural pharmacies average acquisition costs for generic versions were about 2 to 3 percent higher, and for brand drugs were less than 1 percent higher, than costs for urban pharmacies. Due to these relatively low differences, Myers and Stauffer concluded the effect of the difference between the proportion of chain and independent pharmacies that respond to the survey and their proportion nationally was minimal.

[38] The rebate drug product data file contains the active outpatient prescription drugs reported by drug manufacturers for purpose of the Medicaid Drug Rebate Program.

[39] The Drug Efficacy Study Implementation program is a standard used by the Food and Drug Administration to categorize drugs according to their effectiveness—that is, whether a drug demonstrates a health benefit in a real-world situation.

[40] The average wholesale price is the average of the list prices that the manufacturer suggests wholesalers charge pharmacies and is a common benchmark used in pharmaceutical pricing and contracts. The acquisition costs pharmacies pay for a drug are typically less than average wholesale prices.

[41] NDCs are categorized as brand or generic based on the single-source, innovator multiple-source, and non-innovator multiple-source designations from the CMS outpatient drug file. Single-source and innovator multiple-source are categorized together as brand. An override process is used to re-categorize drug versions to reflect reimbursement policy used by the states. For example, an innovator multiple-source version may be re-categorized as generic if it is generally considered generic by states for reimbursement purposes. In some cases where there is a demonstrated variance in prices paid, package size may also be used to define drug groupings.

[42] NADACs are published approximately 6 to 8 weeks after requesting invoices from surveyed pharmacies.

[43] WAC is the manufacturer's list price for wholesalers before rebates and discounts and is published on a weekly basis. Changes in the WAC are measured as the relative percentage difference from the most current published WAC and the previously published WAC.

[44] Myers and Stauffer has performed an analysis of the margin of error associated with NADACs at a 95 percent confidence level—that is, the interval that would contain the actual mean unit costs for 95 percent of the samples that could have been drawn. Based on this analysis, NADACs for nearly all brand versions have a margin of error within plus or minus 5 percentage points of the mean unit cost. On average, the margin of error for all NADACs of brand versions was 0.5 percent. NADACs for all generic versions have a margin of error within plus or minus 10 percentage points of the mean unit cost. On average, the margin of error for all NADACs of generic versions was 2.4 percent. Myers and Stauffer also determined that NADACs for brand drugs are generally consistent with state calculated Average Acquisition Cost (AAC) data. An AAC program is similar to the NADAC program, but on a state level. Myers and Stauffer compared AAC data from Alabama—one of four states with an AAC program at the time—and NADACs. After adjusting for methodological differences such as smaller sample size and biannual surveys of retail community pharmacies, Myers and Stauffer found that the results for brand drugs were not significantly different.

[45] Myers and Stauffer compared NADAC data and state utilization data to calculate the percent of claims reimbursed by Medicaid for which a NADAC had been developed. This analysis found that NADACs had been developed for about 93 percent of all brand-name claims and about 97 percent of generic claims. Myers and Stauffer expect to perform a similar comparison each year to determine the completeness of NADACs and its applicability to state Medicaid programs.

[46] Twenty-seven drugs were not included in our analysis due to either a lack of NADAC or utilization data.

[47] For those 123 drugs, using the single-month PPACA-based FUL would allow states to use the FUL to set their drug reimbursements to pharmacies and allow the FUL to limit Medicaid expenditures, while the 3-month rolling average FUL would not.

[48] CMS publishes the draft single-month PPACA-based FUL files at http://www.medicaid.gov/Medicaid-CHIP-Program-Information/By-Topics/Benefits/Prescription-Drugs/Federal-Upper-Limits.html, accessed June 18, 2013.

[49] An NDC is a unique identifying prescription drug product number that is assigned in part by the Food and Drug Administration and registered and listed with it. See http://www.fda.gov/Drugs/InformationOnDrugs/ucm142438.htm for the Food and Drug Administration's listing of NDCs, accessed November 4, 2013. Each drug may have more than one NDC,

representing different manufacturers and different package sizes. Brand and generic versions of a drug also have different NDCs. The Food and Drug Administration assigns the first segment of the NDC, which identifies the labeler (i.e., the firm that manufactures, repackages, or distributes a drug). The labeler assigns the second and third segments. The second segment identifies a specific strength, dosage form, and formulation (e.g., 20 mg capsules) and the third segment identifies package size and type (e.g., 100 capsules in a bottle).

[50] CMS publishes the draft NADAC files at http://www.medicaid.gov/Medicaid-CHIP-Program-Information/By-Topics/Benefits/Prescription-Drugs/Survey-of-Retail-Prices.html, accessed June 18, 2013.

[51] The 3-month rolling average FUL is the weighted average of the single-month FUL for the current month and the 2 previous months for those drugs with a single-month FUL in all 3 months. For example, the March 2013 3-month rolling average FUL for a drug is the average of the January, February, and March 2013 single-month FULs for that drug. The 3-month rolling average FUL is intended to address problems with month-to-month fluctuations in the single-month FUL. CMS publishes the draft 3-month rolling average PPACA-based FUL files at http://www.medicaid.gov/Medicaid-CHIP-Program-Information/By-Topics/Benefits/Prescription-Drugs/Federal-Upper-Limits.html, accessed August 8, 2013.

[52] CMS officials said they instruct states to use the most recently published FULs for reimbursing pharmacies. For the purposes of our sensitivity analyses, we compared the November 2012, December 2012, and January 2013 single-month FUL data to January, February, and March 2013 NADAC data since these data most likely would have been available for states to use to reimburse pharmacies during first quarter 2013.

[53] We also excluded one drug, polyethylene glycol 3350, from our analysis because it had conflicting unit types in the FUL and NADAC files.

[54] The criteria for establishing a FUL include, but are not limited to, that there be at least three suppliers of a drug that all report and certify AMPs for the drug with a consistent unit type (e.g., tablet). Additionally, the drugs must not be generally considered to be inhalation, infusion, instilled, implanted, or injectable drugs and they must also be fully therapeutically equivalent (i.e., A-rated for therapeutic equivalence).

[55] There were 123 drugs that had a single-month FUL but did not have a 3-month rolling average FUL.

INDEX

A

B

C

D

E

F

Q

R

S